THE

HUNGRY WAR

The Hungry War

AN ACCOUNT OF THE AMERICAN REVOLUTION

by Albert Britt

BARRE GAZETTE
BARRE, MASSACHUSETTS
1961

COPYRIGHT 1961

BARRE PUBLISHING COMPANY, INC.

COMPOSED AND PRINTED IN
THE UNITED STATES OF AMERICA

Library of Congress Catalog Card Number: 61-14611

To Joan and other inquiring youngsters whose
mothers need help in answering questions about this
Revolution of ours

CONTENTS

❖ ❖ ❖

ILLUSTRATIONS

Following page 166

The illustrations are from the collection of the American Antiquarian
Society and are reprinted here with their permission.

viii

Independence was a Fantastic Dream but These Men Believed It and in that Faith They Won the American Revolution and Laid the Foundation of an Enduring Union of States.

Albert Britt
Wellington Farm
Nonquitt, Massachusetts

PROLOGUE

The Shot Heard Round the World

To Americans a chief shrine of Revolution is the sleepy little village of Concord cradled in the rocky hills of Massachusetts about twenty miles northwest of Boston. When the Revolution dawned it was already old as Massachusetts towns go, founded in 1635 when Boston, center of the Puritan world in the new land, could count only five years. A group of settlers newly come from England petitioned the combined heads of the church and state in Boston for a grant of land where two small streams, the Sudbury and the Assabet, came together to form the Concord River. There was rich meadow land along the streams with abudant woodland on the hills for houses and for the fuel to keep them warm on the bleak days of winter. A small tribe of friendly Indians had their camp on Nashawtuc Hill near the junction of the streams. The original grant was six miles square, a typical New England "town." Concord had prospered modestly from the beginning, supplying lumber and firewood to the larger centers of Boston, Charlestown, and Cambridge. In the earlier years all the inhabitants were farmers, even the ministers, school teachers, artisans, and merchants. Population grew and land was set aside for new clusters of humanity: Bedford, Lincoln, Carlisle.

1

Small as it was Concord rated high among the outlying towns. It was here on April 19, 1775, the Yankee Minute Men hastily gathered from Concord and the villages nearby faced British grenadiers — and did not run as the British expected.

For visitors today the greatest interest lies in the statue of the Minute Man by Daniel Chester French, himself a son of Concord. The memorial is unforgetable. The Minute Man stands with one hand holding his musket, the other clutching a plow handle as though reluctant to leave the field of peace for that of war. On the base of the statue are inscribed the well known lines written for that use by Ralph Waldo Emerson, also a citizen of Concord:

> By the rude bridge that arched the flood,
> Their flag to April's breeze unfurled,
> Here once the embattled farmers stood
> And fired the shot heard round the world.

At the opposite end of the bridge, where the British troops formed up to brush the impertinent peasants out of the way, is another tablet set into the stone that marks the grave of two British soldiers killed in the brief flurry of fighting at the bridge. Its inscription is by another Yankee poet, James Russell Lowell:

> They came three thousand miles and died
> To keep the past upon its throne,
> Unheard beyond the ocean-tide
> Their English mother made her moan.

This was only the beginning. Before it ended at York-town in distant Virginia more than six years later many Minute Men and grenadiers had died in a war that few of them wanted. Why then did they fight? And for what? Years later crusty old John Adams remarked that the Revolution had been accomplished in the minds of men before the first shots were fired at Lexington and Concord. Here is a statement that is worth looking into.

To students of an earlier day the causes of the Revolution were simple: George III was a bloody-handed tyrant who with his slavish Parliament insisted on taxing the colonists without giving them the right of representation in the House of Commons. The changes were rung on this simple idea in Fourth of July orations year after year until the belief became a part of the earlier American creed. Only thirty years ago Mayor "Bill" Thompson of Chicago generously offered to give another King George "a punch in the snout" if he were so foolish as to visit that city. Perhaps Thompson thought it was still the same George. In any case he was repeating an old outworn American doctrine.

Wise John Adams knew that the Revolution had begun to simmer under the surface when enough people began to think of themselves as something other than Englishmen who happened to have been born in the colonies. If they were of the third or fourth generation to be born in America the greater was the gap between themselves and the Mother Country. It was their country, not the King's or Parliament's. They had built the ships and the cities, cut away the forests, and fought the Indians. In spite of the paraphernalia of governors and councils the governments that centered in Boston and Philadelphia and Williamsburg were theirs. If those governments were in danger it was for them, the people of America, to do something about it. In that thought was the germ of revolution.

To Parliament, and to the business men in English seaport towns the function of colonies was to provide raw material: timbers to build ships for the royal Navy and merchant marine, hemp for cordage, pitch for calking, tobacco, rice, indigo to fatten English profits. As the colonies grew and trade developed, men in Boston, New York, Philadelphia, and all along the coast were increasingly concerned with profits for themselves. There were tempting cargoes to be had in the West Indies, especially in the Dutch and French islands. Why should they pile up fortunes for English merchants who never saw an American town? The word most often on their lips was Freedom, not Independence: freedom to come and go on their lawful occasions as did their distant English cousins.

CHAPTER I

The Revolution Begins

By 1775 men and women of British blood had been filtering into the New World for over a century and a half. There were more than five generations in Jamestown, New York, Plymouth, Massachusetts Bay. Individuals were sifting through the passes of the Alleghenies into the valley of the Tennessee, to Kentucky and the Ohio country. The tide was running westward and the British dream of profitable trading posts along the seaboard was emptier than even the colonists knew.

The first charter of Virginia, signed by James I, April 10, 1606, holds in its old-fashioned phrases an indication of the purpose of the venture. It was in substance a grant of the right to establish trading posts, called "plantations," in America made to a group of commercial minded gentlemen in London who were prepared to invest money, of course in the hope of a good profit. The merchants of London were familiar with trading companies. They were operating them successfully in the hide and timber trade with the countries around the Baltic Sea in the north and the Black Sea in the south, and the British East India Company, destined for greatness, had recently been launched. Many of the gentlemen now proposing to try their luck in an American enterprise had done

well for themselves in the trade with Russia and the Scandina-
vian countries. For their purposes the boundaries of Virginia
were very liberal indeed, being approximately equal to the entire
Atlantic seaboard of North America. They extended from 34°
N. Lat. to 45° N. Lat., or from about the southern line of
North Carolina to the northeastern tip of Nova Scotia. Our
thrifty ancestors dealt generously, if vaguely, with large slices
of empty American land which few of them would ever see.

The long stretch of seacoast was to be divided between
two groups of "gentlemen adventurers," as these speculators
were called. Known as the London Company at the south and
the Plimouth Company in the north, the groups overlapped
two degrees, more than a hundred miles, at the middle. To
insure the necessary monopoly of trading operations other settlements were required to be at least fifty miles distant from
posts already established.

The three ships bearing the first settlers to Jamestown,
Sarah Constant, Discovery, and *Goodspeed,* left London late
in December 1606 with a hundred and twenty prospective
"planters," of whom sixteen died on the voyage out. The hundred and four who survived were a sorry lot; men out of
debtors jails; restless, shiftless riffraff, although most of them
had declared themselves "gentlemen." Worse choices for settlers in the savage American wilderness could hardly have been
made. The men who were to lay the foundations for Virginia
aristocracy came later. There were no women on these first
ships. By the end of the first year only fifty-three were left
alive; malaria, starvation, and Indians had taken care of the
others. But a beginning had been made.

Incidentally by this time the French in Canada were
already reaping a rich harvest in the fur trade and, fifty years
before the first shabby huts were built in Jamestown, the
Spaniards had called into being a flourishing civilization in

Mexico with a university, printing presses, and many churches; and Pizarro had annexed the gold and sliver hoards of the Incas in Peru. It is also worth noting that for all the ambitious hopes of the backers of the first English planting in the New World, not a cent of profit was ever received by them.

In spite of the shabby hopelessness of those first years at Jamestown there were a few men who cut down trees, planted crops, fought Indians, and managed to survive. They were the ones who understood the redoubtable Captain John Smith when he said that he who does not work shall not eat. It was in those early years, the "starving time," that John Rolfe brought tobacco seed from the prosperous fields of Cuba with the knowledge of the best way to cure and ship the weed. When that happened civilization was on its way in Virginia.

It was thirteen years after the first landing at Jamestown that another pathetic handful of refugees found a foothold at Plymouth, and another ten before the Puritans landed in what is now Boston. (The Puritans of Boston are not to be confused with the Pilgrims of Plymouth. The former sought to "purify" the established Church of England from within; the the latter to get away from the established church and all its forms and works. Also the Puritans included many people of means in England with goods and gear; the Pilgrims had no capital and precious few goods.)

For all of them, whether in Massachusetts or Virginia, the ties of blood with England were close, however much some of them might chafe and strain. But England was far away, four or five weeks of stormy voyaging at the best; and as generations passed the bonds became steadily weaker. To farmers in Massachusetts and planters in Virginia the memory of a homeland was dim and distant. A hundred years after the first settlers landed in Massachusetts Bay generations rather than weeks lay between these English in America and their cousins in England. After 1650 the flow into the New World slackened and England was but a tale told by a few old men and women. To the active colonists the chief concern was with their own immediate environment: planting, reaping, trading, building. They were of British blood, but their interest was in the new land. They no longer thought of themselves as English, although they were not yet Americans. Pressed for identification they spoke of themselves as Yankees, New Yorkers, Virginians.

They had their own newspapers, schools, churches, colleges — seven of them, laws, and customs. They were largely self-governing, acknowledging allegiance to the King but conceding little right or authority to Parliament. Even if new laws of trade were announced from London the requirements were usually easily evaded or modified in practice. Parliament had grown steadily in power, especially after the Glorious Revolution of 1688 when they asserted their power to force Catholic James II into exile and chose Mary, staunch Protestant daughter of James, with her husband Dutch William as joint sovereigns. James II had lasted long enough to make an attempt to consolidate the New England colonies for more efficient and economical administration. The New England charters were cancelled by royal decree and Massachusetts, Rhode Island, and Connecticut were combined with New York under the royal governorship of Edmund Andros. This might have been a wise move at the right time, but it was too late for that kind of wisdom. The Yankees had been running their own affairs too long to permit anyone to push them around. James slipped off to Holland on his way to restless exile in France and the colonists heaved a sigh of relief.

For nearly seventy years England was busy with European matters and the new Americans were free again to follow their own new American ways with their own legislatures and judges. The King might still appoint Royal Governors, often American-born, but the colonies paid the Governor's salary, not always promptly; and while the Home Government might sometimes veto colonial laws the process took several months in the doing and a few changes in the old law would set everything to rights. William was Stadt-holder of Holland in addition to being part-time King of England and he was more interested in resisting the pretensions of Louis XIV of France to the headship of Europe than in joining in a disorderly and fruitless scuffle with a handful of American colonists. The war of the League of Augsburg which followed was King William's War to the colonists, a significant distinction. Those upstart Americans were developing a geography and a history of their own and their own way of looking at things with their own eyes.

Next came the war of the Spanish Succession, Queen Anne's War on this side of the Atlantic. The ending of Queen Anne's reign left England without an heir to the throne. This time Parliament looked further into Europe than Holland and found a great grandson of a daughter of James I of England in the person of George Elector of Hanover. Now appears the first of the House of Hanover to reign over England. This George thought little of his new honor. In fact he didn't even bother to learn the English speech. Little Hanover was good enough for him. He disliked English food, English beds, English women, and his feeling about the dour island climate was beyond words — even German words.

This was better than Parliament had dared hope. George had no stupid ideas of ruling the English. Someone else could do that. Hard-headed, hard working, and hard drinking Robert Walpole became Prime Minister and held office for twenty years. He was corrupt and dissolute, but he knew his people and he had a shrewd common sense. He gave England time

to rest from the heavy losses of the European wars and time
to look about. He also gave the colonists time in which to
become more conscious of their own strength and their ability
to govern themselves. Urged to lay more taxes on them Walpole refused. "I have half of England against me already," he
said. "Should I have the colonists too?"

In spite of Walpole's warning there was a pointless Euro-
pean war in 1745, King George's War to the Americans, the
War of the Austrian Succession to European courts and chan-
celleries, and to the indifferent English the War of Jenkins'
Ear.* For some reason, chiefly hatred for the French and
Indian raiders who hovered along the northern borders, the
Colony of Massachusetts raised and equipped an expedition of
their own against the French fortress of Louisbourg on Cape
Breton Island. The affair was planned by Governor Shirley,
a popular Royal Governor, and commanded by a Yankee merchant William Pepperell. The attack violated all the rules
of warfare — but it succeeded — and the French Gibraltar
of America was in Yankee hands. Unfortunately the British
in the Treaty of Aachen that concluded the war handed Louisbourg back to the French in consideration of French abandon-
ment of claims to Madras in distant India. The British agreed
to recompense Massachusetts for the cost of the adventure and
made Mr. Pepperell a baronet, but the men who fought at
Louisbourg were not happy over the outcome of their glorious
enterprise.

Generally speaking, for all their growing sense of an
American destiny, there was little community of feeling
among the colonies in their relations with each other. Roads
were few and bad and communication was uncertain. Travel

---

*Jenkins, an English sea captain, appeared at the bar of the House of Com-
mons and displayed an ear cut off by a Spanish officer who had boarded
his ship. The House of Commons showed no interest in a war with Spain
and took no action.

was slow and painful and the wayside inns were usually worse than uncomfortable. Colonial distances can be roughly computed by substituting days for hours in terms of modern rail travel. They were thirteen separate entities, speaking the same language to be sure, but showing little interest in the aims and troubles of each other. In 1754 there was a meeting of delegates from seven of the colonies at Albany, New York, called at the suggestion of the Lords of Trade to consider ways of improving the relations of these distant portions of the Empire, especially with the Indian tribes who were growing increasingly restless. A Plan of Union drawn up by Benjamin Franklin was submitted to the conferees. Here was the germ of what might some day be a nation. The Plan proposed the creation of a central body, an American parliament, to deal with matters that concerned all of them. Local matters could be left to the individual colonies. All were to pledge allegiance to the King.

It was a wise, farseeing plan. If it had been approved and put in operation there might have been no Revolution — at least no violent one. The colonial assemblies unanimously rejected it because it gave too much power to the King. Parliament turned it down because it conceded too much to the colonies. And so the mills of the gods continued to grind.

In 1756 England and France found themselves at war again. In Europe it was the Seven Years War known to the colonies as the French and Indian War. This war brought the new Americans to a fuller realization of their own needs and possibilities. They had already come a long way from Jamestown and Massachusetts Bay.

Now a greater man than Walpole became head of the British government; a man who dreamed of empire, the elder Pitt, later to be the Earl of Chatham. He was the first English statesman since the days of the great Elizabethans to visualize the larger world outside the wearisome squabbles of Western Europe and the British Isles. The French were trying for a foothold in India and held all of Canada north of the English colonies. There was Pitt's empire ready for the taking and he meant to have it. This was the first of the world wars fought all over the globe: India, North America, the continent of Europe. At the end the empire had gone from dream to reality.

The taking of Canada was a godsend to the settlers in New England and northern New York. No longer would they cower in fear of sudden raids by French and Indians down the Connecticut or along Lake Champlain. The nightmares that had haunted them for a hundred years were lifted and the skies were clear. This had been their war as well as a war of the British. In Massachusetts fifteen per cent of the able-bodied men were under arms. In New Jersey taxes in support of the war amounted to $5.00 per capita for the total population.

There had been other fighting fronts than those in Canada. In Virginia an able, humorless young planter named George Washington had led the Virginia militia to hold back the Shawnees along the Ohio. He had taken his Virginians into the frenzy of killing that is remembered as Braddock's Massacre where they had fought the Indians in Indian style, fanning out among the trees and making their shots count. The British didn't think much of this kind of fighting, but they were to meet it again in the years ahead. They would hear more of George Washington too.

Back in England there was rejoicing over the final victory, of course, but there was also rueful counting of the cost. As nearly as could be estimated at Whitehall the English were seventy-five million pounds in debt for the war in America — nothing in these days of astronomical spending but a huge

burden in the eighteenth century. How should it be lifted?
It was George Grenville, Chancellor of the Exchequer and
later Prime Minister, who saw the answer to that question. It
was the American colonists who had benefited most by the
successful outcome. To them the peace along the border meant
that the families on the frontier could clear away the forests,
plant their crops, and sleep without uneasy dreams of fire and
slaughter in the darkness. To be sure colonial soldiers had
fought alongside British regulars; fought well and many had
died. But they had benefited directly in material ways,
through the sale of supplies to the troops paid for with British
gold. Some of them had earned a thrifty penny or two trading with the French in the West Indies, as had British merchants. Profit seems to acknowlege no national allegiance.
All in all, the colonies had had the best of the bargain in every
way. Why should they not help to pay the bills?

But there was a catch in the plan. What seemed reasonable and fair in London seemed unthinkable in Boston. Crude
as the colonists may have been in many ways, they knew about
taxes. They had paid them before, but then they had been
levied by their own legislatures, voted by representatives of
their own choosing. Now taxes would be fixed by Parliament
without so much as by your leave. The old explanation that
the colonies rebelled against taxation without representation
is too simple. What they objected to was taxation by Parliament. If their own representatives had sat in the House of
Commons they would still have objected. The levying and
collecting of taxes by some body of men in distant England
was vastly different from taxing themselves and they would
have none of it. The sin of Grenville and Parliament was ignorance of the men they were attempting to govern, the greatest
sin that legislators and administrators can commit.

There had been royal taxes before, such as the tax in

1733 on sugar and molasses brought from the West Indies to make rum for Yankee drinking, for the Indian trade, or for the slave trade overseas. Domestic drinking in New England was considerable, to the great annoyance of the straitlaced clergy. When the frame of Jonathan Edwards' new meeting house was raised at Northampton, Massachusetts, that worthy man had observed with dismay the quantity of rum and hard cider that had lightened the labor. The sugar tax was heavy: sixpence (about ten cents) a pound — or it would have been heavy if the shippers had paid it. Smuggling was easy. The tax collectors found it more comfortable to look the other way when the boats came in. Sometimes the collector failed to make the long, disagreeable voyage to his post of duty but stayed comfortably at home in England, drawing his pay with commendable regularity.

Now it was clear that the British intended to collect the taxes. They needed the money. The day for evading and postponing was past. The old sugar law was rewritten soon after the end of the Seven Years War. The new rate was only half that of the old, but this time it was to be paid; the British saw to that. And a small tax that is paid is more grievous than one twice its size that is easily evaded. The palmy days of smuggling were over.

Great as was the annoyance caused by the tax on sugar and molasses it was nothing compared to the indignation aroused by the Stamp Act of 1765. That is a form of taxation that governments like, collected in advance. The payer buys the stamps from the government and pays for them in money out of his own pocket. Britain was stretching a long arm across the Atlantic and helping herself to the taxpayers' slender store of specie. Stamps were required on every printed document: deeds, bills of sale, receipts, contracts; and on every piece of printed matter: newspaper, pamphlet, broadside.

Harvard diplomas called for stamps to the value of two pounds sterling. The people of Massachusetts Bay were highly articulate both in speech and print and the tax on newspapers outraged them. This was really a tax on thinking and as such it was not to be borne. There were riots in Boston and elsewhere. Offices where the stamps were on sale were broken open and the sheets scattered about the streets. Andrew Oliver, Secretary of the Province and brother-in-law of Thomas Hutchinson, was hanged in effigy, his house broken into and its contents thrown into the street. A few nights later another mob attacked Hutchinson's house and sacked it from top to bottom.

Hutchinson was the Lieutenant Governor, doomed also to be the last Royal Governor, and at the same time Chief Justice. He was of long New England ancestry, a descendant of the Anne Hutchinson who had been driven out of Boston because she had questioned the authority of the heads of church and state. But this Hutchinson was a person of means and distinction, high in the confidence of the Government party, an aristocrat in manner and way of life. He had warned the authorities at Whitehall against the indiscreet taxes, as had Governor Bernard, but the men who sat in comfortable chairs at massive desks in London knew better. The mob knew nothing of these warnings; they knew only that these were Government men and as such fair game. Hutchinson was to die in exile in England mourning for his pleasant country home on Blue Hill in Milton.

Out of this hurly burly of riots and looting came one good thing, a call for representatives of the colonies to meet in New York for consideration of their common grievances. That was the Stamp Act Congress. The tone of their deliberations was moderate and reasonable. They declared their allegiance to the King and their desire to serve him in all just respects. There was no hint of rebellion or of separation from the mother country.   These were men of British blood claiming their rights under the British constitution.   They were not alone in their protests.   Such Englishmen as the elder Pitt, Burke, Fox, Shelburne, Halifax spoke out for the colonists in Parliament. Burke warned the House of Commons that they could not profit from trade with the colonies and at the same time lay and collect taxes that tended to destroy that trade. "You can not have it both ways," he said.

For once the Government listened to good advice and the stamp tax was repealed; by this time it was evident even at Whitehall that few stamps were being sold and English merchants complained that trade with the colonies was at a standstill.   The repeal was a concession but a grudging one.   There were other taxes, on sugar, tea, cloth, men's hats, all things of daily use.   The colonists were accustomed to these as a necessary part of the British practice of trade control.   So the merchants of Boston, New York, and Philadelphia settled back into their customary routine.   Nothing seemed farther from their minds than independence, and war was unthinkable.

There was one exception to this general attitude of tranquility.   Samuel Adams of Boston, tireless agitator against British tyranny, turned his wrath against his fellow countrymen and warned them that the end of their troubles was not yet. Sam was an exception any way we look at him.   He was the son of a hard working family, a distant cousin of John who was now practicing law, a graduate of Harvard, and a failure in business — a cardinal sin in that time.   His father, a successful brewer and a deacon in the church, had advanced the funds needed to set young Samuel up in business.   The latter promptly loaned half the money to a partner and, when profits failed to accrue, capital and partner both vanished.   Sam had little trouble losing the rest.   At one time he was tax collector and handled the details of his office so badly that he was accused of embezzlement. Once he tried his hand at garbage collecting. Of his performance in that useful but malodorous post there is no record.

Incompetent as he was by ordinary standards, there was one thing that he could do supremely well. He could influence the minds of men. And he knew men; not the respectable, ambitious men who naturally leaned to the Government side, the side of law and order — and opportunity. The men Adams knew were the shipworkers, the longshoremen, the artisans, men in the raw. He walked the streets tirelessly, pausing to chat with workers here and there, asking questions, dropping hints. He knew that there were vastly more of these roughly dressed people than there were riding in carriages and dining at mahogany tables in the big houses. They might not vote — that was for men with property enough to qualify. But these men could swing cudgels, if need be carry guns, and in the long run they would have their way if they were carefully led.

In the Boston Town Meeting Adams found a forum and a sounding board, although he was no orator. His style was rather that of simple, almost humble exposition and argument, with an occasional touch of piety which was not assumed. His was the profound and sincere religious faith of the older New England mold; he liked to call himself the "last of the Puritans." He was a busy and inflammatory newspaper writer, and the target of his declamations was always the same: the sins and the sinister aims of the British Government. He instituted Committees of Correspondence in the other colonies and made his letters powerful engines of unrest.

The Adams clan in New England was a numerous one and for good reason. The first of the name in America had eight sons and, according to the record, "several" daughters.

His eldest son had twelve children and his eldest son in turn also had twelve.

Sam was an enigma to his cousin John, the thrifty, ambitious young lawyer concerned to make adequate provision for his growing family. Samuel too had a family, but he seemed to give little thought to the morrow except to shape another dart for the British. But there was another side to John. He too loved liberty along with order and sound government, and this prompted him to write once of Sam: "Adams, I believe, has the most thorough understanding of liberty and her resources in the temper and character of the people, though not in the law and constitution; as well as the most habitual, radical love of it of any of them, as well as the most correct, genteel, and artful pen."

Not all the men that Samuel influenced went clothed in homespun and wore heavy shoes. There was John Hancock, for example. He had inherited a fortune from his uncle Thomas, and had added to it until now he was the richest man in Boston, proud of his fine clothes and his magnificent carriage. By all the logic of circumstance and social position Hancock should have allied himself with the merchant aristocrats on the side of the Royal Governor. But he was a trader with the sugar growers of the West Indies and with the wine producers of the Portuguese islands and the new taxes fell heavily on him. He had political ambitions too and he thought that slovenly Samuel could help him to gratify them. Whatever his reasoning may have been it was clear that he was strongly on the patriot side.

Of course all good Government men hated Adams, especially Thomas Hutchinson, Royal Governor—and still Chief Justice. It was Hutchinson who said of Adams: "I doubt whether there is a greater incendiary in the King's dominions or a man of greater malignity of heart, or who less scruples any measure ever so criminal to accomplish his purposes; and I think I do him no injustice when I suppose that he wishes the destruction of every friend to government in America." But Hutchinson knew also that this man whom he hated so bitterly was not to be bought or dazzled by favor or position and he warned the British that "such is the inflexible disposition of this man that he would never be conciliated by any office or gift whatsoever."

If there was any one man who launched the American Revolution it was this footless, slovenly, impecunious Sam Adams. How far in advance he saw the inevitable end of the road he was traveling is any man's guess. As late as August 1774, Benjamin Franklin, then in London as colonial agent, recorded in his diary the substance of a statement he had recently made to Lord Chatham: "I assured him that having more than once traveled almost from one end of the country to the other, and kept a variety of company, eating, drinking, and conversing with them freely, I never had heard in any conversation from any person, drunk or sober, the least expression of a wish for a separation, or a hint that such a thing would be advantageous to America."

Years later John Quincy Adams, son of John, a delegate to the peace conference at The Hague that ended the War of 1812, notes in his diary that Sir James Mackintosh, a British delegate, asked him how many Americans had seriously desired separation. "I said, 'perhaps my father, Samuel Adams, and James Otis.'"

Samuel Adams may be an enigma among Bostonians, but there was good reason for the colony on Massachusetts Bay to take the lead in the assertion of colonial rights. On August 26, 1629, a year before the founding of the colony, a small group of men in the town of Cambridge in England signed a document known as the Cambridge Agreement, a "True

Coppie" of which still exists. After stating their willingness to lead the way in establishing a colony in the New World the signers added: "Provided always, that before the last of September next the whole government together with the patent for the said plantation be first by an order of the court legally transferred and established to remain with us and others that shall inhabite upon the said plantation."

The names signed to this document are interesting. The first is that of Richard Saltonstall, an ancestor of the Massachusetts Senator. Others are John Winthrop, many times Governor of the little community, Thomas Dudley, curious combination of ecclesiastic and business acumen, William Vassall, successful merchant and one time British Minister to Denmark, Isaack Johnson, son-in-law and estates manager of the Earl of Lincoln. These were Puritans, but neither refugees nor rebels, whatever King Charles thought of them.

Among them were men skilled in the drawing of contracts and leases, at home in the world of seventeenth century business and politics, who had noted the slow starvation of Jamestown and were of no mind to repeat this in Massachusetts. When they sailed they would take with them the charter of their liberties and the men to whom the charter had been issued. Here was the germ of a self-governing and strong willed dominion in the Western wilds.

A hundred and fifty years later in that same Massachusetts, a prosperous, proud, stubborn colony, events moved steadily in the direction of separation. Continued disorder in Boston might or might not be traceable to the hand of Samuel Adams working in and through the Boston Town Meeting, but in due course the riots brought their reward. If the Bostonians could not control their own hoodlums then the British must do it for them — with troops. In October of 1768 soldiers appeared on the streets of the staid old town and sentries walked their beats, challenging respectable citizens as they plodded wearily home after a hard day at desk or counter. Of course there was trouble and in March 1770, came the Boston "Massacre." As massacres go it wasn't much. Schoolboys bombarded a sentry with icy snowballs and troops came to his aid. A crowd gathered to watch and to jeer the "lobster backs," as the redcoats were being called. The details are still unclear. The fact was that shots were fired by soldiers, with or without orders, and three of the jeering onlookers were dead on the snow. Two others died later of their wounds.

In the trial that followed there was evidence that the provocation of the soldiers was extreme and it seemed that in the circumstances men and officers had borne themselves well. As a part of the atmosphere of good will that respectable Boston attempted to create John Adams and young Josiah Quincy defended the soldiers. They were acquitted, but the mischief had been done. Blood had been spilled and by no means all of Boston was respectable. Of course the future was uncertain, but men still hoped.

The pot simmered for another three years, but townsmen and soldiers eyed each other with mutual distrust. To the men of the town the troops were the minions of British tyranny, and to the soldiers the townsmen were miserable rebels lacking only arms and the courage to use them to make trouble for the guardians of order. The next stage in the growing tension was the opposition to the tax on tea. That needs a little explaining. The British East India Company, a powerful influence in British policy, found itself with an overload of tea which must find a market. To the British mind the solution was simple: sell it to the colonies. It wasn't as simple as the British thought. To be sure the colonials were tea-drinkers; coffee was scarce and high in cost. But if the East India Company were to be saved it must have a monopoly of the trade in America. So agents were chosen to sell the tea to the housewives. In most of the towns the sale of tea was an important item in the daily dealings of the small shop-keepers; Dutch tea as often as British, filtered in by way of the Dutch islands in the West Indies. Now the little shop-keeper was out in the cold. Another blunder was written down on the growing list of official errors. Individuals refused to drink the official beverage even though it was offered at a much lower price than they had been paying. Evidently the heads of government in England had never heard the old saying, "You can lead a horse to water, but you can't make him drink," especially if the drink is East India Company tea.

The tea ships came to every important port from Boston to distant Charleston. Various things began to happen. In Charleston the cargoes were stored in damp cellars where the tea soon mildewed. New York refused to permit the landing of the precious boxes and the ships sailed away disconsolately. Boston was more spectacular. The ships were at the wharves and unloading was about to begin when an unexpected crowd of workmen, clad in a rather feeble imitation of Indian costume, often daubs of paint and a few feathers, appeared to take over the job. Now the historic Boston Tea Party got under way. It was a cold day in late November of 1773. The work went forward rapidly and with order. Only the tea was touched and that went over the side and Boston harbor became a gigantic tea pot. Officers and crew were unharmed, merely pushed out of the way. No damage was done to the ships, only to the tea. Then the imitation Indians went back into their places as workers in the shops and shipyards of Boston.

The busy hand of Sam Adams was to be seen in this business of course. It was just his kind of trouble. As soon as the ships had sailed into the harbor placards had appeared on walls and trees:

Friends! Brethren! Countrymen! That worst of plagues, the detested tea shipped for this Port by the East India Company is now arrived in the Harbour; the hour of destruction, of manly opposition to the machinations of Tyranny, stares you in the Face; Every Friend to his Country, to Himself, and to Posterity, is now called upon to meet at Fanueil Hall, at nine o'clock this day, at which time the bell will ring to make united and successful resistance to this last, worst, and most destructive measure of Administration.

Boston, Nov. 29, 1773

This was an unpardonable act from the British point of view. The government had been defied and the property of British subjects destroyed. The tea was valued at eighteen thousand pounds sterling. The port of Boston was closed, which meant that no ships were permitted to move in or out. The customs house was moved to Salem, and hard times came to the people of Boston. While the prime offense had been given in Boston, excitement spread rapidly through the colonies and supplies for the beleagured city came from as far away as South Carolina. In Williamsburg, Virginia, Colonel Washington spoke with characteristic brevity and point: "If need be I will raise one thousand men, subsist them at my own expense, and march myself at their head to the relief of Boston." At least the Bostonians would not starve and, what was more to the point, the people of the different colonies were beginning to find something in common. What had happened in Boston had meaning all along the coast line down to the southern extremity of British authority.

The logical next step to the Tea Party was more troops. British authority had been challenged and the vandalism on board the ships was almost an act of war. General Gage was summoned from New York to take command, and by the middle of 1774 four regiments were in Boston and more were being readied. These country bumpkins must be taught who were their masters. Orders were that the householders of the town provide quarters for the officers and, if possible, the men. But the town was overcrowded and four regiments, even of reduced strength, take a lot of room. Troops found themselves living in tents on the Common well into November — not a comfortable place when a cold nor'easter blows off the bay.

The British gave signs of a desire to be friendly and conciliatory. Thomas Gage, the commander, had been a captain with Braddock and had seen Virginia militia stand and fight when British regulars broke in panic flight. He had married an American born girl and she made friends in Boston. In general the troops behaved well in spite of small provocations. Of course the younger officers, and most of them were young, blew off steam occasionally, as young men will in a strange new land. Taverns and grogshops abounded in Puritan Boston and there was the usual horseplay to top off a convivial evening. Once a thickheaded countryman aroused much amusement by trying to bargain with a soldier for the latter's musket. This poor soul was tarred and feathered and carried in procession, but to the younger British this was only good clean fun. Some of the sober ones on both sides took uneasy note of these proceedings, but such rough play was at least better than war. They counseled caution and hoped for the best.

In the meantime a call went round the colonies for a meeting of representatives in Philadelphia in September 1774, for the discussion of their mutual problems. This meeting went into the records as the First Continental Congress. In Boston, General Gage sought to prevent the election of delegates to Philadelphia by ordering the place of the local meeting to be shifted to Salem — then to make doubly sure cancelled the meeting altogether. The members met in spite of Gage, and Samuel Adams locked the doors and put the key in his pocket.

Five delegates to Philadelphia were chosen and another meeting arranged for. When news of this action reached England, George III exclaimed: "I am not sorry that the line of conduct seems now chalked out. The New England governments are now in a state of rebellion; blows must decide whether they are to be subject to this country or independent." The blows would be heavier than King George could guess.

The First Continental Congress brought together the most notable body of men that assembled anywhere in that century. All forms and degrees of opinion were represented. The extremists Samuel and John Adams, both now pressing for separation since no acceptable alternative seemed possible, joined with such other radicals as Stephen Hopkins from Rhode Island, Richard Henry Lee and Patrick Henry from Virginia, with moderates like George Washington and with conservatives such as John Jay of New York and Joseph Galloway from Pennsylvania. Galloway fought for his pronounced Loyalist position through the meeting and afterwards. In the face of a growing demand for bold action he presented his Plan of Union which would have set up a Colonial Parliament with power to deal with purely colonial affairs. Whatever its merits it was forestalled in the Congress by news of the Suffolk Resolves passed by a convention held in Suffolk County, Massachusetts, and proclaiming the virtue of disobedience to the so-called Coercive Acts aimed chiefly at Massachusetts. The forthright character of this local declaration broke the strength of the moderates and conservatives and gave the balance of power into the hands of the extremists.

After disposing of Galloway's Plan of Union the Congress went on to adopt a Declaration of Rights and Grievances aimed at influencing public opinion in England. This document led Lord Chatham to declare that "for solidity of reason, force of sagacity, and wisdom of conclusion under a complication of difficult circumstances, no nation or body of men can stand in preference to the general Congress at Philadelphia." If England had had enough Chathams a federation of British dominions might well have been formed then and there, instead of a hundred years later, but wise men are always too few. The time for conciliation and mutual adjustment was running out.

Chatham was not the only prominent Englishman to speak out in behalf of the Americans. In Parliament Irish-born Edmund Burke, Charles James Fox, just beginning his meteoric career, Lord Shelburne and Lord Halifax spoke powerfully in behalf of the colonists. Chatham was blunt and forthright in his declaration to Parliament: "If I were an American, as I am an Englishman, while a foreign troop was landed in my country, I never would lay down my arms! Never, never, never." In April of this critical year of 1774, the Duke of Richmond, a wealthy landowner, said in the House of Lords: "I wish from the bottom of my heart that the Americans may resist and get the better of the force sent against them." Prominent officers in the Army and Navy refused to serve against the colonists. Two shining examples were Jeffrey Amherst in the Army and Admiral Keppel of the Navy. Both were men of undoubted courage and competence. Amherst had commanded British forces in America during the Seven Years War and knew the quality and temper of the Americans better than most Englishmen.

George III turned a deaf ear to objections and warnings, especially after he found a willing and effective tool in Lord North as Prime Minister. It was the King's unhappy fate to be a strong believer in absolute monarchy at a time when the power of Parliament was beginning to overshadow the throne. He was far from being the bloody-handed tyrant the Americans were describing him. In reality he was a patriotic Englishman, a model of domestic bliss and personal conduct. His mother, wearied by the dissolute and faithless behavior of her husband the Crown Prince, devoted her full time and attention to the young Prince. "George, be a King!" she urged him and the young King tried. Unquestionably many useful lessons may be learned at a mother's knee, but political philosophy is not among them.

Boston, for all her distress as an occupied city, was still one of the large and prosperous centers of American life. There were only three others to be considered: New York, Philadelphia, and Charleston in South Carolina. It was also a center of intellectual life. Harvard College was established in 1636 and by 1775 was regarded as a necessity for the sons of well to do families in the colony. Both Samuel and John Adams were graduates. Samuel was eighteen when he was graduated. Three years later he returned for a master's degree, taking an affirmative position on the question, "Whether it be lawful to resist the Supreme Magistrate, if the Commonwealth can not be otherwise preserved." That was strong medicine for the peaceful Boston of 1743, when he said it.

Boston harbor was large and well sheltered with deep water for safe anchoring and plenty of wharf space for loading and unloading the many ships that came and went in normal times. No wonder the overseas trade was large. The town itself was practically an island built on three hills, surrounded by tidal flats (now the Back Bay) and the Charles River. To the south was Dorchester Neck, a narrow neck connecting Beacon Hill and the others with the main land. It was over this neck of land that the farmers' carts came to market with supplies for the housewives of Boston. What is now East Boston was then Noddles Neck. Strung around were small villages that were offshoots of the original settlement: Watertown, Belmont, Newtown (now Cambridge), the various Newtons that make up the present city of Newton, Dedham, Somerville, and the rest.   Farther out were two villages that were soon to become better known: Lexington and Concord.

The population figures for that time are mostly guess-work.   It was widely believed that there was a scriptural prohibition against numbering the people, which made census statistics a bit difficult. Fifteen thousand for Boston would be a fair estimate.   On the slopes of the three hills there was much open space and the Common existed much as it is today.

Here then is a rough picture of the town that was soon to be the stage of a portentous drama.   The time was early in 1775 and unrest was growing.

CHAPTER II

The Day of Lexington and Concord

April 19, 1775, was a clear bright day and farmers were
about early. It had been a mild winter and an early spring
for New England, and farm work was well advanced for the
season. But another kind of work was in hand for this day.
For some time word had been filtering through to the British
that stores of ammunition were being gathered in the villages
around Boston and that the militia were unusually active,
drilling long hours frequently instead of waiting for the annual
training day, as had been the custom. The British held the
colonial militia in low esteem and officers were of the opinion
that a single company of British grenadiers could send a regiment of Minute Men running madly in all directions.

Here and there an officer smelled danger in the air. Before any powder had been burned in action, Lord Percy wrote
to his father, the Earl of Northumberland: "What makes an
insurrection here always more formidable than in other places
is that there is a law of this Province which obliges every in-
habitant to be furnished with a firelock, bayonet, and pretty
considerable quantity of ammunition." The same Lord Percy
saw a threat too in some of the colony's ministers. "I am sorry

29

to say that no body of men are so injurious to peace and tranquility as the clergy. They preach sedition openly from their pulpits."

The young man could have been thinking of Jonathan Mayhew in Boston or William Emerson in Concord. In early April Emerson had preached from the text: "Behold God himself is with us for our captain!" His hearers were warned not to start trouble, but to be ready for it if it came. "Arise! my injured countrymen, and plead even with the sword, the firelock, and the bayonet. Plead with your arms the birthright of Englishmen, the dearly purchased legacy left you." Emerson's manse still stands in Concord not over a hundred yards from the bridge where the far-resounding shots were fired on the day of the battle, and he watched the action from his window.

Other clergymen did not hesitate to speak out. In his Thanksgiving Day sermon the fall after the Concord fight, the Reverend Samuel Baldwin in another Massachusetts town thanked God that there was "sufficient hemp in the colonies to hang all the Tories." In general the German Lutherans in Pennsylvania, a key state, stood aloof as far as they dared, but after the Continental Army came into being the Reverend Peter Muhlenberg, *Teufel Piet* to his people, told his congregation that "in the language of Holy Writ there was a time for all things — a time to pray, — but that those times had passed away, and there was a time to fight, and that time has now come." Then he threw off his ministerial gown revealing a Continental uniform of buff and blue, as a drum beat sounded at the door of his church.

The young officers with Gage might be pardoned for their ignorant innocence, but some of the older men, including Gage, had seen colonial troops fight well against the French and Indians in the Seven Years War. They at least should have remembered. Dieskau the Frenchman had seen Massachusetts militia come against him in the fighting around Lake George and recorded what he saw. In the morning they fight like good boys, he said, "at noon like men, and in the afternoon like devils."

General Gage in Boston decided that the arsenals of powder and arms must be broken up; especially noted were those in Lexington and Concord. Lieutenant Colonel Smith was put in command of the demolition force which was made up of units from grenadier and light infantry regiments, crack regiments well trained in the European style of fighting, close order, shoulder to shoulder, firing by volleys and then rushing in with the bayonet. It was not to be like that this pleasant April day. The colonials were as well informed as the British of what was being planned and had messengers waiting to carry the news when the march began. The name of Paul Revere is almost as familiar to American children as that of George Washington. It was arranged that lanterns should be shown in the belfry of the Old North Church:

> One if by land, two if by sea,
> And I on the opposite shore will be
> Ready to ride and spread the alarm
> Through every Middlesex village and farm.

Here is a point on which history needs amending. Revere rode as Longfellow said in his poem, but he was not the only messenger on the road that night. A man with the unromantic name of William Dawes started at about the same time by way of Brighton Bridge and the Concord Road, and in the end went farther than Revere who was stopped by mounted British skirmishers just outside Lexington. Dawes dodged the British and kept on to Concord. Why has he been so carefully ignored in the literature of the period, especially by Mr. Longfellow?

The reason is given in a little known bit of verse by a minor poet of Longfellow's time Helen F. Moore:

> 'Tis all very well for the children to hear
> Of the midnight Ride of Paul Revere,
> But why should my name be quite forgot
> Who rode as boldly and well, God wot?
> Why should I ask? The reason is clear—
> My name was Dawes and his Revere.*

The reason for the neglect of the man with the unromantic name goes a little deeper than an accident of nomenclature. For Dawes the ride that night was a high spot in an otherwise commonplace though by no means wasted life. He may well have been among the defenders of the redoubt on Breed's Hill and it is certain that he served for a time with the Continental Army. Later he appears as a groceryman in Worcester where he was also a commissary agent by Congressional appointment. Exciting as the night ride must have been for Revere, it was in reality only an incident in a career of considerable distinction. He was one of the best known silversmiths and engravers in a time that was prolific of much beautifully designed and executed silverware. To own a piece of Revere silver today is in itself a mark of distinction. On one occasion he even designed and built a set of false teeth, an impressive combination of screws and springs, for no less a person than George Washington. This dental equipment might well have been responsible for the grim look that Washington wore for his portraits.

For all the speed and attempted secrecy with which the British set out for what some of the young officers regarded as a day of fun at the expense of these stupid yokels, thanks

---

*With grateful acknowledgment to Clarence F. Brigham's introduction to his collected *Paul Revere's Engravings*.

to Revere, Dawes and the grapevine telegraph of the countryside, the villagers were warned in time.   A third man became
an inadvertent bearer of the news that the British were coming.   Samuel Prescott, a young doctor in Concord, was returning from a late call on a young lady in Lexington when he
encountered the horsemen who had taken Revere.   By hard
riding and skilful dodging he got away to join Dawes in warning the people of Concord.   Young Dr. Prescott was not
marked for long service in the American cause. He appeared
briefly with the Massachusetts militia at the capture of Ticonderoga.   Soon after he shipped on one of the early Yankee
privateers out of a Yankee port.   Taken by a British frigate
he was sent to Halifax with others in the crew and died in
jail there, probably in 1777.

Men with arms in their hands were soon gathering in
Lexington and Concord.   Lexington was first on the way and
was only a slight diversion.   Colonel Smith sent Major Pitcairn
with four companies, at most two hundred men, probably less.
In Lexington they found about eighty militiamen gathered on
the green under the nominal command of Captain John Parker,
a veteran of Wolfe's capture of Quebec in that other war. Fifty
years later his grandson, the Reverend Joseph Parker, one of
the front rank fighters for the Unitarian doctrine, quoted
Captain John as having cautioned his men as they stood in
ragged line awaiting the British: "Don't fire unless you are
fired on, but if they want a war it might as well begin here."

The record of what happened in the few minutes that the
fight on the Lexington green lasted is obscure and confused.
Did Major Pitcairn shout: "Disperse, ye rebels! Damn you,
why don't you disperse?"   Some remembered that Pitcairn
fired his pistol, others that the first shot was fired by a British
private, still others that an officer ordered a volley. Shots were
fired, a few by the militia, the troops rushed forward with

bayonets fixed, and the militia scattered. One wounded colonial was dispatched with a bayonet thrust as he lay on the ground. Eight of the Americans were killed, seven of them Lexington men. There were no casualties among the British, and that was the battle of Lexington. In the Lexington town hall there is displayed a pair of long barreled pistols, believed to have been the property of Major Pitcairn, picked up along the road to Concord after the fight. It was only a six mile march to Concord and it was still a bright warm April day.

There were distinguished visitors in Lexington the night before that the British would have been delighted to gather in, the pernicious Sam Adams and his friend and ardent supporter John Hancock. Here were the makers of revolution ripe for the picking. Warning was sent to the home of the Reverend Jonas Clarke where the two had been spending the night and they slipped out the back door and away through the fields to safety. When the firing broke out in Lexington they were still in sound of it and Adams exclaimed: "Oh, what a glorious morning is this!" Hancock the practical business man assumed that he spoke as one interested in farming and wondered at this new quirk in the old plotter's complicated nature.

The flurry at Lexington had been only a brief pause in the march to the real objective which was Concord, proving only what the British already believed, that these colonials would not stand up to British soldiers. Probably the same thing would be true at Concord. What they sought there was not a fight but powder and guns. The arms were there. On that score the British information was correct. Foragers had been busy all spring gathering supplies wherever they could find them and storing them around the village. They even "lifted" cannon from carelessly guarded British fortifications on Boston Neck, ten six-pounders, three twenty-four pounders. When warning came of the British march the cannon were lifted off their carriages and buried under the rows of sage in Mrs. Barrett's garden. Bullets were hidden in the bottom of a barrel of goose feathers stored against need for new pillows. The communion silver from Mr. Emerson's church was dropped in a barrel of soft soap. The farmers' almanacs that year of omen had carried recipes for the making of gunpowder, always in demand in all the colonies. The villagers worked fast in the little time they had and the British found little to reward them for their long march — a few rusty old muskets and ninety to a hundred pounds of powder. Officers complained later that many of their men got out of hand and improved the opportunity to do a little general looting. There was some random shooting, perhaps the result of a swift raid on the local tavern's supply of rum. An old house on the main street in Concord bears the name of the Bullet Hole House and shows the hole as evidence.

Meanwhile what of the Concord Minute Men? While the people of the village had been busy stowing the contraband ammunition out of the invader's sight Minute Men had been gathering from Concord and surrounding towns, Lincoln, Acton, Chelmsford, Bradford, Carlisle. Colonel John Barrett was in nominal command, an elderly man so lame that he found walking difficult. The field command, if there was such a thing, was largely an accident of the moment. While the cheerful shooting and looting around the town went forward the Minute Men gathered on the far side of the little stream dignified by the name of the Concord River behind the North Bridge, one of the two bridges that spanned the stream. It is mildly interesting that the church from which the signal to Revere had been flashed should have had the same name as the bridge in Concord where more history was soon to be made; interesting but purely coincidental.

Word was soon sent to the British headquarters in the

Wright Tavern and Captain Laurie was ordered to assemble
enough troops to scatter the waiting militia, who were under
orders to hold their fire until the British attacked. The troops,
about a hundred, came carelessly down the gentle slope to the
bridge beyond which the Minute Men huddled. Estimates of
the number of militia range from a possible four hundred to
an absurd fifteen hundred. There was no plan of battle except
for the British to attack and the militia, presumably, to run.
Smoke rolled up from the village where the wreckage of carts
and gun carriages was being burned and Joseph Hosmer called
out: "Will you let them burn the town?" Troops were already
beginning to tear up the planks of the bridge and the Minute
Men moved forward threateningly. At this a volley of shots
came from the British side and at least one American dropped
with a bullet through his head. The Minute Men stood their
ground stoutly and returned the fire. Three or four of the
troops fell wounded, at least two of them fatally. These were
the men who were buried near the bridge:

> They came three thousand miles and died
> To keep the past upon its throne.

Then the British unaccountably and hastily withdrew and the
Battle of Concord, at least that phase of it, was over. There
was the final act of this drama to be played, the long agony
of the march back to Boston.

There are occasional questions as to the reasons for the
term Minute Men. Legally the militia comprised all the able
bodied men of the colony. Not long before the Concord affair
colonial authorities, probably local Committees of Safety, in-
structed the captains of companies to select from each company
a special group of the ablest, and usually the youngest, to be
prepared to march at a "minute's" notice, suitably armed and
equipped. This was in effect an elite corps whose responsibility

it was to meet the first shock of attack. When the war began in earnest the term soon ceased to have any significance.

Late in January 1775, a hundred Minute Men drilling at Concord had taken an oath asserting that there was no slackening in their allegiance to the King:

> First, that we whose names are hereunto subscribed will to the utmost of our power defend His Majesty King George the Third, his Person, Crown, and Dignity.
>
> Second, that we will at the same time to the utmost of our power and abilities defend all and everyone of our Charter Rights, Liberties and Privileges, and will hold ourselves in readiness at a minute's warning with arms and ammunition thus to do.
>
> Thirdly, that we will at all times and in all places obey our officers chosen by us.

Why did the brief and apparently pointless scuffle at the bridge echo so fast and so loudly through the colonies and turn so many eyes to this little New England village? That is easily answered. Raw farmers fresh from the plow, crudely drilled and armed, had stood up to disciplined British troops and answered back to bloody effect and the farmers had held the field. Now the government in London could know that Americans would fight, if they had the wit to read the writing on the wall. The sword had been drawn and war had begun.

Concord was a small village in 1775 and it still is. There are still bright days in April and farmers still work the stony fields, probably not so many as in that other April. Fields have gone back to woodland and the little town is more a suburb of Boston than a remote settlement. Many of the old houses remain, the Bullet Hole House, the Manse where the Reverend William Emerson looked through an upper window to see the dawn of Revolution. The Wright Tavern stands where it stood then and not far away is the church where the Provincial Congress of the state met, to the embarrassment and annoyance of the British.   Concord had had its one big day and it treasures its legends and its memories.

Among the revolutionary tablets and memories of Concord there is one that has nothing to do with war and battle. On what was once a hillside farm in the outskirts of the village there is a stone bearing this inscription:

> Ephraim Wales Bull planted seeds of a wild Labrusca grape found growing on this hillside which after three generations through his work and wisdom became in this garden in September, 1840, the Concord grape.

And that too is worth noting.

Now the drama of that April day begins to unfold.   Farmers, artisans, shop-keepers had been gathering all morning, not in Concord but along the road by which the troops must march on their way back to Boston, twenty miles of it.   Practically all the colonials had arms, chiefly muskets and a few fowling pieces.   Buckshot can be deadly at close range.   Stone walls lined the road, ideal cover for snipers, and there were houses, boulders, trees.   It was made to order for what was to come.   These men had guns and could use them.   They were not the marksmen that Ethan Allen and Daniel Morgan led, but this was close range.   Men slipped from wall to wall and stone to stone, keeping pace with the soldiers who were soon near panic. "Why won't these blasted scoundrels stand up and fight like men!"   In his report to General Gage three days after the disaster Lieutenant Colonel Smith, commander of the expedition, made this complaint: "Notwithstanding the enemy's numbers, they did not make one gallant attempt during so long an action, though our men were so very much fatigued, but kept under cover."   This was no dress parade stuff, no occasion for gallantry, but deadly killing.   The war had really begun. When Revere mounted his horse on the Charlestown side Dr. Joseph Warren, stout patriot fated to die at Bunker Hill, turned to his few companions and said: "They have begun it. That either party could do and we will end it. That only we can do." Truer words were never spoken, but it was to take eight hard years to reach victory and the Treaty of Paris.

How many militiamen gathered along the road that day? There is no record. One young British officer thought there were at least a thousand to the mile. Twenty thousand Minute Men to speed the enemy on their way? Hardly likely or possible. Few or many, there were enough. At one point in this death march a narrow bridge crowded the soldiers into a trap. Amos Barrett saw the shambles there from behind a stone wall nearby and wrote to a friend afterwards: "A grait many lay dead and the road was bloddy." This might have been at Monotomoy — sometimes Monomoy, now Arlington — where a marker makes queer boast:

> On the 19th. of April, 1775, more were killed on both sides within our limits than in any other town; at least 22 Americans and probably more than twice that number of British fell in this town.

Relief for the hard pressed British came just in time. Young Lord Percy, he who had written forebodingly of the possibilities of war in the colony, met the British near Lexington with fresh troops as the forced retreat was about to turn into a disorderly foot race and covered them the last stage to safety in Boston. An officer who was probably a participant in the rout wrote later: "Thus ended this expedition which from beginning to end was as ill-planned and as ill-executed as it was possible to be. Thus for a few trifling stores the Grenadiers and Light Infantry had a march of about fifty miles through an enemy country, and in all human probability most every man would have been cut off if the brigade had not fortunately come to their assistance, for when the brigade joined us, there were very few men who had any ammunition left, so fatigued that we must have surrendered."

Reports of the losses in this running fight vary widely. For the British, General Gage's official report showed seventy-two dead while unofficial estimates ran as high as 273. Militia losses were given as eighty-eight killed, wounded, and missing. Gage's figures seem small in view of the admission that the British were on the verge of complete rout when Percy brought the brigade to their rescue, but 273 is obviously high. The militia were not riflemen, as were the frontiersmen, and they were armed with muskets of notorious inaccuracy at ranges over fifty yards. So were the British, for the matter of that. Whatever the losses Massachusetts opinion held that it was a low price to pay for the privilege of driving crack British troops along the road to defeat.

Obviously the British knew little of the geography of the country around Boston. Captain Laurie who commanded the British at the bridge in Concord gave a report that was incoherent and contradictory as well as inaccurate. For example he speaks of passing through the village of "Anatomy," certainly Monotomoy, and also Roxbury and Medford on the march to Concord, a geographical absurdity. He also makes mention of the scalping of fallen soldiers by the savage colonials. That was highly unlikely. Frontiersmen who were much in Indian country sometimes followed the Indian custom of collecting those gruesome trophies, but these were villagers, most of whom seldom saw an Indian.

Word that raw militiamen had driven grenadiers like sheep spread fast through the colonies. Israel Putnam, Connecticut farmer, Indian fighter, and trapper, heard it and left his plow in the furrow. Sending word to the militia commanders of the colony, he rode fast to Cambridge, a hundred miles in eighteen hours without change of horses. This was only the first fight; there would be more and he wanted to be in them. In Virginia Patrick Henry stirred the House of Burgesses at Williamsburg: "Our brethren are already in the field! Why stand ye here idle? Is life so dear and peace so sweet as to be purchased at the price of chains and slavery!" South Carolina heard the news and men began to move.

In the Continental Congress meeting in Philadelphia the news of Lexington and Concord brought a swift and surprising result. John Adams of Massachusetts, crabbed, suspicious John, staunch patriot and lover of the liberties of Massachusetts, urged the choice of George Washington as commander in chief of a Continental Army. Washington sitting in the same meeting heard Adams and may well have wondered. Massachusetts choosing a man from Virginia; a Yankee lawyer praising a Virginia aristocrat who was probably the richest man in all the colonies. Adams was no fool. He knew that New England could not fight this war alone. Virginia was the largest and most powerful of the colonies and without her there would be no Revolution south of the Potomac and very little anywhere else.

Washington was the best known leader who could have been chosen. He had been with Braddock in the fatal ambush along the way to Fort Duquesne in the Seven Years War, and with his Virginia militia had covered the rout of the British veterans and saved the bleeding remnants in retreat. Through the war he commanded the militia along the western frontier and came out with the rank of colonel. The British had reason to know him. Once he had ridden all the way to Boston to lay his complaints before General Shirley, commander of the Britsh forces in the colonies. An English captain had refused to recognize the superior rank and authority of a militia colonel. That was important when the colonel was serious, hard headed, dignified George Washington. Shirley recognized the justice of the colonel's claim and the captain was whipped into line. We may be sure that John Adams liked him none the less for that show of stubborn pride. He too was proud and stubborn.

There was only one drawback to his appointment as the head of the Continental Army: there was no such army and no money in the treasury with which to pay for one. There never was enough — ever. Besides the colonials had no liking for the idea of a national army. That was the British way. Each of the thirteen colonies had its own militia. Why wasn't that enough? It had served at Lexington and Concord, hadn't it? The question of pay for his services didn't bother Washington. He could serve without pay and did, all the way through. Washington fought the Revolution for his "board and keep," as the Yankees put it. His expense accounts were as carefully kept as those of his farms in Virginia and Congress paid them, but seldom promptly. The final total was $64,000. When Adams' motion was adopted the new commander spoke a few words of dignified acknowledgment to Congress and set out for Cambridge where the militia were gathering. Now the squabble of a mob of countrymen with a handful of British troops was becoming a full dress war.

CHAPTER III

Bunker Hill and the Siege of Boston

The fiasco of the long march from Concord to safety in Boston ended the British efforts to clear away the fringe of hostility that was closing in on them. For all their boasted superiority in arms the crack companies of grenadiers and light infantry were helpless against the sharp jabs delivered by the colonial militia from the shelter of stone walls, boulders and trees. This was not the way gentlemen fought in Europe, but these were not gentlemen; they were farmers and village people fighting in defense of their homes — and of something more that they hardly understood yet.

While the militia gathered at Cambridge British officers in Boston fumed over the bad manners and deplorable morals of the colonials. A rumor ran through the streets of a plot to kill all the British officers who could be reached and an unknown officer wrote in his diary: "What a set of villains they must be to think of such a thing! But there is nothing, be it ever so bad, that these people will not think of to gain their ends." This rumor went wherever idle rumors go and others took its place, equally baseless.

In London Dr. Samuel Johnson, self-apppointed final arbiter on all things, spat his venom against the colonials of

whom he knew nothing: "Sir, your people are a race of con-
victs. Has not America always been our penal colony? Are
they not smugglers? I am willing to love all mankind except
an American. How is it, sir, that we hear the loudest yelps for
liberty from these people who are themselves the drivers of
negroes?"

Of course, the British argued, the root of the trouble is
that they aren't gentlemen. That was true, by English standards. Wilderness air did not agree with English aristocrats.
Major Caldwell, an officer at Quebec in the Seven Years War,
was vastly amused by the sort of human beings who held commissions in colonial regiments. "Of those we took one major
was a blacksmith, another a hatter; of their captains, there
was a butcher, a tanner, a shoemaker, a tavern-keeper, etc.,
yet they pretended to be gentlemen." Of course there was
Washington, owner of land and slaves. He might almost have
been English so lifelike was his imitation, but that made the
puzzle only the harder to solve. The Reverend Jacob Duché
in Philadelphia, first chaplain of the Continental Congress
but a staunch Loyalist, wrote to Washington expressing his
surprise that that good churchman should have among his
officers so many men whom he would hardly think of inviting
to dinner. A look around at some of the staff increased this
mystification — Henry Knox a bookseller in Boston, Benedict Arnold a New Haven merchant and real estate speculator,
Nathanael Greene a Rhode Island blacksmith and a Quaker to
boot.

Events moved swiftly after Lexington and Concord.
While Gage's forces huddled in Boston the militia gathered at
Cambridge to block the crossing of the Charles. Greene came
fast from Rhode Island followed by three companies of fighting Quakers. Ethan Allen and John Stark brought their riflemen from Vermont; Daniel Morgan took his men up from

the Shenandoah valley. Here was a man to remember, a hard drinking, hard fighting, fast moving mountain man who had been a wagoner for Braddock and had felt the lash of a British whip for the offense of knocking a British officer from under his hat. Five hundred lashes there were, at least so tradition said. Tradition was probably only partly truthful for anything approaching five hundred lashes was a punishment that even the strongest could hardly take and live. Morgan not only lived but boasted that he counted every stroke and that the tally was short by one; he still owed the King that one stroke. Whatever the number of strokes he marched with his ninety-six quick stepping mountain men the six hundred miles from Winchester, Virginia, to Cambridge in twenty-one days.

Cambridge was wide open to British attack from across the Charles River that curled aimlessly around Boston. It's still the same sluggish stream seeming to go everywhere and nowhere, winding through marshes and around low hills, now a highway for canoes on lazy summer afternoons. The Charles was both a defense and a menace to the Americans. If it was to be an effective defense more was needed than a peaceful river. Bunker Hill was the answer. The battle that was fought there on June 17 was from the strict military point of view a comedy of errors. To begin with the correct name of the hill up which the British marched to the attack was Breed's and not Bunker's, as historians beyond number have pointed out. Whatever the name the militia set to work with spade and mattock and axe to dig trenches and throw up earthworks on the crest of the hill that commanded the slope up which the British were expected to march. There were fifteen hundred militia against two thousand to twenty-five hundred British, well trained and disciplined troops. Since the day of the Concord fight General Sir William Howe had arrived to take over the active command of the British.

HMS *Cerberus* which brought Major General Howe to Boston on May 25, 1775, brought two other major generals: Sir Henry Clinton, destined for many long weary days in New York, and John Burgoyne, "Gentleman Johnny," who was to bow off the stage at Saratoga. Three "top brass" officers in one ship suggested that someone in England was beginning to have serious thoughts about these American rebels. A rhymester in England with a sense of humor summed it up in these lines:

> Behold the *Cerberus* the Atlantic plow,
> Her precious cargo — Burgoyne, Clinton, Howe,
> Bow, wow, wow!

When the war was somewhat older Lord North, cynical, good natured Prime Minister of England freed his mind about them in characteristic fashion: "I do not know whether our generals will frighten the Americans, but they certainly frighten me."

Who was in command of the militia against this glittering array of imperial might? Artemas Ward, a veteran of the French and Indian War, had been appointed Commander in Chief of the militia of the colony by the Massachusetts Provincial Congress. It was he who had directed the building of the defense works on one or both of the hills near Charlestown commanding the Charles River, although he remained at his headquarters in Cambridge on the day of the fight. Who determined that the placing of the redoubt should be on the lower and more accessible of the two hills? Possibly Putnam who wanted nothing so much as to get a shot at the British. A rival of Putnam for the honor of chief field command was William Prescott a farmer near Pepperell, Massachusetts, and a veteran of two wars: King George's War and the French and Indian War. Prescott was a man of commanding stature easily singled out from men of average height. There is a story that in the midst of the bombardment that preceded the assault this tall figure could easily be seen moving about quietly among the militia apparently calming and encouraging the raw troops. In Boston Gage, watching from a housetop, pointed out Prescott to Abijah Willard, a Boston merchant, asking the name of the colonial officer and whether he would fight. Willard answered: "That's my brother-in-law William Prescott. I can not answer for his men, but Prescott will fight you to the gates of Hell!" Prescott as much as anyone commanded the Americans that day.

The troops were ferried across the river in rowboats and landed on the narrow beach at the foot of the hill to form up for the charge. It was a clear warm day with little wind. The attack was in the very best miltary tradition. Up the hill the troops marched, shoulder to shoulder, bayonets fixed, officers in front, their drawn swords flashing in the sun. At the top of the hill the Americans crouched in the trench, scarcely so much as a hand showing above the wall of earth. As the British came on, Putnam, a tough Connecticut farmer, passed the word along the line: "Don't fire till you can see the whites of their eyes. Aim for the white crossbelts!"

It was like shooting at sitting ducks, unsportsmanlike but deadly. At close range it was hard to miss, even with muskets. Gaps opened in the solid British line as the attack halted and then fell back. Such withering fire was more than they could take. At the foot of the slope the officers whipped them into line again and led them back to the charge. A second attack was sent reeling down the hill now dotted with the bodies of British dead and wounded.

Colonial powder, never plentiful, had given out and the British got in with the bayonet at the third try as the survivors streamed back to Cambridge. The British could claim a victory on paper, but the price they had paid was a dear one:

1,040 dead to the militia total of 449. Niney-two of the British dead were officers. Small wonder that Greene remarked drily that the colonists were willing to sell a number of hills at the same price. When he heard the news wise Benjamin Franklin summed up the matter tersely: "Americans will fight; England has lost her colonies forever."

William Cheever, an American Loyalist, saw the battle from a housetop in Boston and recorded what he saw in his diary: "A large number of Regulars (2 or 3,000) commanded by G'l Howe were boated over to Charlestown today to dislodge the Provincials of a hill which they had intrenched on; this they did and set the town of Charlestown on fire. The Engagement was very warm whereby a great many are killed and wounded (10 or 1100 of the Regulars) a melancholy Scene of Fire and Slaughter." A lieutenant in the King's Own made even briefer report of the battle in which he took part: "Between 3 and 4 o'clock in the afternoon after an obstinate resistance drove the Rebels from their Redout and a Breastwork and from thence made them fly quite over the Neck which joins Charlestown to the Continent."

The attempt at Concord had failed and the capture of Bunker Hill had been at best a dubious bargain. There were to be no more such speculations. The next event was the arrival of George Washington who set about the hard task of building an army among people who knew only colonial militia. There was no treasure chest of war and no disposition to provide one. Congress had authorized the new Commander in Chief to organize an army and train it. Such idle details as material, human and otherwise, means or methods, were evidently not the concern of Congress. The task was herculean and the time was short.

Washington had little patience with bunglers and laggards and he had his full share of both. He lashed out in a letter to his half-brother John Augustus: "Such a dearth of public spirit and such a want of virtue, such stock-jobbing and fertility in all the low arts to obtain advantage of one kind or another in this great change of military arrangement I never saw before, and I pray God's mercy that I may never see again." Nevertheless he was to see the same and worse many times before the war ended. The truth was that the people of New England distrusted a professional army as an unworthy imitation of British tyranny. Their militia had stopped the British at Concord and again at Bunker Hill. Now let the other colonies do as well. Even John Adams who had proposed Washington for the post was lukewarm in his support of the idea of a national army. The very name Continental Army was an offense in colonial eyes.

Only a few days after choosing Washington as commander of a non-existent army Congress had given ample demonstration of this muddle-headedness in military affairs by approving a wild plan hatched by Benedict Arnold for an attack on Quebec, the Gibraltar of North America. It was to be a two-pronged enterprise with Richard Montgomery leading about a thousand men north along Lake Champlain to capture Montreal, then marching down the St. Lawrence to meet Arnold with a similar force for a combined attack on Quebec. Montgomery had been an officer in the British Army and after the Seven Years War he resigned his commission and became an American farmer near Albany. Now he was an officer of colonial militia with the rank of brigadier general. His part of the joint task was accomplished with comparative ease after a late start and many delays. Montreal fell and Montgomery, leaving a considerable portion of his force for the garrisoning of that post, marched down river toward Quebec.

It was Arnold who had the trouble. His route was up the Kennebec River through the wilderness of Maine to the head

of the river near the northern boundary of the province, then a
long carry over to the Chaudiere and down that river to the
St. Lawrence near the coveted fortress; six hundred miles of
backbreaking work. The season was well advanced and winter
was near at hand when the clumsy bateaux in which the men
expected to pole their way against the current to the Height
of Land were ready. The river grew shallow as they advanced
and men waded waist deep over slippery boulders pushing and
pulling their leaky boats. As winter came on and the cold
grew more bitter desertions increased and only six hundred
men finally struggled over the twelve-mile portage to the Chaudiere. With them were Dan Morgan the rifleman and most
of the ninety-six men who had followed him north from Virginia.

It was near the end of December when this ragged, hungry
remnant met Montgomery and his depleted force before Quebec. The French-Canadians, the *habitans,* who had been
expected to rally to the aid of the Americans for revenge
against the hated British had failed to appear. Much as they
may have hated the British they hated fighting more, and they
especially hated the thought of fighting in the snow and the
cold of the Canadian winter. It was only the men who had
come all the way with him that Arnold could add to Montgomery's force for this forlorn hope. The enlistments of many
of them were expiring on January first, so if Quebec was to
be taken there could be no waiting.

On New Year's Eve of 1775 these men marched through a
blinding snow storm to attack the strongest fortress in the
whole of North America. It was a foredoomed attempt but it
seemed for a moment to be succeeding. Then Montgomery
was killed, Arnold wounded, and Morgan captured by the British. Arnold and his handful of survivors held on in the villages
near by until spring and then made their way back by Lake

Champlain. It was a wild, hopeless idea of course, but it might just have succeeded. If it had the British position in that part of the continent would have been precarious at the time when there was need that it be most secure. Even as it was, British authorities long remembered that night of peril in the darkness and the snow and strengthened their Canadian forces in consequence.

Back in Cambridge meanwhile Washington had arrived and set about the organizing and drilling of an army. The spot where he took over is marked by a tablet inscribed:

> Here stood the Washington Elm under which George Washington took command of the American Army, July 3, 1775.

He had brought no troops with him for the good reason that there were none to bring. The "American Army" was only a hope. But he did have a small staff, including two former British officers, General Charles Lee and Horatio Gates, names that were to be heard again and not always pleasantly. And he had a flag, thirteen stripes to represent the thirteen colonies, with the crosses of St. George and St. Andrew in the corner, an improvised combination of the old and the new that was hoped for.

The new commander's obstacles were many and baffling: the unwillingness of members of colonial militia to enlist, even for a year, a lack of ammunition, guns, and clothing; food was often scanty, and there were few tents. Then there were the willing blunderers. In a letter to Joseph Reed, a member of Congress, Washington apologized for the blots: "I had just finished my letter when a blundering Lieutenant of the blundering Captain Coit, who had just blundered upon two vessels from Nova Scotia, came in with the account of it, and before I could rescue my letter, without knowing what he did, picked up a candle and sprinkled it with grease."

Cannon were needed for the siege of Boston which had now begun and there were no cannon. The Minute Men had done pretty well in lifting a few from the ill-guarded forts on Boston Neck and burying them in Mrs. Barrett's garden in Concord, but now British sentinels were more watchful and that road was closed. But there was artillery gathering rust and cobwebs in the embrasures at Fort Ticonderoga which Ethan Allen had taken early in the year.

Brief and bloodless as it was the capture of Ticonderoga found a well deserved place in the catalogue of tradition. The fort was an important guardpost between the headwaters of the Hudson River and Lake Champlain. It was taken by Allen and his Green Mountain Boys supplemented by eighty-three Massachusetts militia led by Benedict Arnold. The legend goes that when Allen hammered on the gate of the fortress on May 10, 1775, the sentinel inside demanded to know in whose name he was being challenged to open the gate, to which Allen replied: "In the name of the Great Jehovah and the Continental Congress!" At least that's the way it appears in his official report written some time later. There is another version allegedly by an eye-witness. This quotes Allen as shouting up to the commander of the garrison who was slow in appearing: "Come down, you old rat!"

It was far from Ticonderoga to Boston and the problem of transport was a tough one. Henry Knox, late a Boston bookseller now an artillery officer, solved it. He gathered many yokes of oxen and dragged the cannon all the way down from Ticonderoga and the length of Massachusetts to help in the siege of Boston. Motorists now travel swiftly over the General Knox Highway which follows the road that Knox and his men had cut through the Berkshires. As they roll they may read the markers that tell the story, twenty-seven of them, all alike:

> "Through this place passed Gen. Henry Knox in the winter of 1775-6 to deliver to General George Washington at Cambridge the train of artillery from Fort Ticonderoga used to force the British army to evacuate Boston."

Fortunately for them the British still held the approach by sea, and when the Americans began to show signs of a plan to storm the forts that guarded the landward approach General Howe decided that enough was enough, loaded his troops on transports and sailed on March 17, 1776, for Halifax, taking with him as many Boston Loyalists as the ships would hold. Massachusetts observes Evacuation Day as a school holiday, but to many of the present day citizens the fact that it is also sacred to St. Patrick is perhaps more important.

Before the British ships had cleared the mouth of the harbor Washington was preparing for the hard task of shifting his embryonic army to New York, an obvious target for the British. This was a time of testing for the militia who were so proud of their performance in the fighting around Boston. How would they meet it? The results were mixed. Men like Putnam, Greene, and Knox would go wherever there was need, Arnold wherever there was the chance of a good fight. Many of the militia balked at the transfer. They would serve only under officers of their own choosing. They had already been too long away from their farms and their families and they were needed to put in new crops. The war could wait. Even some of the general officers, men whom Washington had trusted, pleaded pressing business at home. Enough went to make a respectable showing, including a number of hardy fishermen from Gloucester, men who knew the sea and boats. They were to be useful more than once.

The shifting of the action from Boston to New York and New Jersey marked also the beginning of a new kind of war. From April 19, 1775, to March 17, 1776, the conflict could be called a civil war in which a comparatively small local body of disorderly rebels sought to evade and defeat the orders of the proper authorities—who were of course the British troops in Boston aided and upheld by what the British firmly believed was a majority of the rightminded citizens who sought only to restore order. The appointment of Washington, a Virginian, as Commander in Chief of a Continental Army was a strong hint that something more was in the making, but the bewildered British dismissed it as an empty gesture. That these misguided people should defy the Might, Majesty, and Power of Britain and attempt to withdraw from the old relationship of mother and daughter was unthinkable.

There was reason enough for the British attitude. Here were three million people more or less, beads strung on a slender thread that stretched nearly eighteen hundred miles from end to end, challenging the British Empire. In the other war, twenty years earlier, British strength had overthrown the France that fifty years prior had claimed the dominance of all Europe and had come close to proving it. Now France was out of Canada and her tentative hold in India had been broken. Then there was the British Navy, mistress of the seas with the greatest fleet of merchant ships in the world to carry men and supplies to the subduing of a handful of rebels. Surely the colonial dream of freedom from the Mother Country was but the delusion of a few maniacs.

What was there on the other side? There was distance for one thing, three thousand miles from the mouth of the English Channel to the scene of the war — five weeks of hard sailing and more for ships in convoy. Frederick the Great of Prussia, probably the master strategist of the age, looked at the map and found the odds against the British. They might win battles, but they would surely lose the war. Time was on the side of the rebels, he said.

Then there was the topography of the country, a narrow strip of settled land along tidewater, then a wilderness of forest and mountain cut by rivers to complicate the movement of men and supplies. It was largely unmapped country with few towns to serve as bases, poor country for the carrying on of complicated campaigns but ideal for irregular warfare, as would be proved when the time came. It was not only the American people but also the American land that the British must subdue.

CHAPTER IV

Independence and Defeat

In spite of all the obstacles Washington did not linger long at Cambridge after Boston was evacuated. On March 18 the first units of the new army started for New York, where they would find themselves fighting alongside troops from New Jersey, Pennsylvania, and even distant Maryland and Delaware. The regiments from Maryland and Delaware were to fight through the war and leave an indelible mark on the war records of the time for valor and endurance. The sight must have set some of the men from Massachusetts, Connecticut, and Rhode Island to thinking that this was no longer a gathering of Yankee militia, but something resembling a national army. The commander of one Massachusetts regiment, Loammi Baldwin, also fought through the war, witnessing the surrender at Saratoga, and then immortalized his name by developing the Baldwin apple. This fruit, along with the Concord grape, has long since become an American standby.

The war was less than a year old but Americans, starting from scratch, had penned a British army in Boston and then starved them out. They had won no battles, but they had made the enemy pay a bitter price for small successes. Now the Redcoats were out of New England and the army was pushing hard for New York. Perhaps they might take heavy toll for British victories there too. The talk around the camp-fires may well have been almost cheerful.

Events were moving fast in the field; did the Congress meeting in Philadelphia realize how fast? States were beginning to act; New Hampshire, South Carolina, Virginia, and New Jersey adopoted constitutions and set up in business for themselves. Virginia's opened with a "declaration of rights of the good people of Virginia, assembled in full and free convention," drafted by patrician George Mason, an authentic aristocrat even by English standards. The first paragraph lays down a philosophy of the relation of the individual to government that was to have a profound influence:

> That all men are by nature equally free and independent, and have certain inherent rights, of which, when they enter into a state of society, they cannot by any compact deprive or divest their posterity; namely, the enjoyment of life and liberty, with the means of acquiring and possessing property, and pursuing and obtaining happiness and safety.

Now Congress began to take stock of the realities of the time. Two days before Virginia adopted her sweeping declaration, another Virginian, Richard Henry Lee, offered a resolution in the Philadelpha meeting: "That these United Colonies are, and of right ought to be Free and Independent States." On Lee's motion a committee was appointed to prepare a formal declaration, "setting forth the causes which impelled us to this mighty resolution." There were five men on the committee, Thomas Jefferson, John Adams, Benjamin Franklin, Roger Sherman, and Robert Livingston. The committee acted swiftly and on July 4, 1776, their report was adopted. This was the Declaration of Independence.

The Declaration was not adopted without opposition and debate. John Dickinson, whose "Letters from an American Farmer" had seemed to put him among the extreme radicals, spoke powerfully against it, warning his fellows that they were condemning their countrymen to wretchedness and death; but once the die was cast he acquiesced in the result and enlisted in the Continental Army as a private.

The document adopted that July the Fourth deserves much more space than can be given it here. The story goes that Jefferson suggested to John Adams that he undertake the writing of it, but Adams promptly passed the task back to the man from Virginia, saying, according to his own recollection, "You are a Virginian and a Virginian ought to appear at the head of this business. I am obnoxious, suspected, and unpopular; you are very much otherwise. You can write ten times better than I." Jefferson's memory of the incident did not agree with the Adams version, but John may well have been right. At least there is no doubt, no matter what each said to the other, that it was Jefferson who did the writing; and the ringing challenge of the phrases proves that the choice was a wise one. Adams and Franklin suggested a few slight changes in the wording and a sentence denouncing negro slavery was eliminated as too controversial. The original draft, preserved by Jefferson, is in the Library of Congress and its margins show the notations of B. F. and J. A.

Of course there was criticism. A few complained that he had borrowed both ideas and phrases. This moved Jefferson to brief reply. In a letter to Henry Lee he said: "Neither aiming at originality of principles or sentiments, nor yet copied from any particular and previous writing, it was intended to be an expression of the American mind . . . . All its authority rests on the harmonizing sentiments of the day, whether expressed in conversation, in letters, in printed essays, or in elementary books of public rights, as Aristotle, Cicero, Locke, Sidney, etc." Many readers felt to their own surprise that this man had said exactly what they had been thinking all along. Perhaps the Declaration was not yet quite the American mind as the author had said, but it soon became so.

The Declaration is one of our sacred documents, probably more praised than read, viewed by many as an instrument of government on a par with the Constitution. In reality it was propaganda, unpopular as that word is these days, a reassuring message to the governments of the continent of Europe, especially to France and Spain, saying to them: Be not disturbed. This is not a revolution sending kings into exile, upsetting thrones, and spreading discord and anarchy through the world. Because of the respect we have for your good opinions we are letting you know that we are acting within our rights in separating ourselves from the mother country. Since most of the Continental powers feared and hated England they were more than willing to be reassured.

Read the Declaration through carefully from the opening: "When in the course of human events," to the concluding phrase:

> And for the support of this declaration, with a firm reliance on the protection of divine providence, we mutually pledge to each other our lives, our fortunes, and our sacred honor.

This was not only propaganda but propaganda in the grand manner. To be certain that there was no misunderstanding of his motives and his purpose Jefferson recited the long drum roll of charges against the King, rather than Parliament, as the chief author of their grievances. "He has long repeated," "He has refused," "He has forbidden," "He has called together," "He has dissolved," "He has endeavored," "He has obstructed," "He has erected," "He has combined." So the list runs on, monotonous and powerful in its repetitions, all aimed at the King as the bond of empire with whom they had made an agreement which he and he only had broken.

For all its concilitary gestures to the kings of Europe there was high explosive in the second paragraph of the Declaration, although it has attracted little attention. Read it now.

> We hold these truths to be self-evident, that all men are created equal, that they are endowed by their Creator with certain unalienable rights; that among these are life, liberty, and the pursuit of happiness; that to secure these rights governments are instituted among men, deriving their just powers from the consent of the governed; that whenever any form of government becomes destructive of these ends, it is the right of the people to alter or to abolish it, and to institute new government, laying its foundations on such principles and organizing its powers in such form, as shall seem to them most likely to effect their safety and happiness.

The phrase "life, liberty, and the pursuit of happiness" has been much discussed. What does the pursuit of happiness have to do with life and liberty? The Virginia Bill of Rights mentions it as an incident to the acquiring of property, and in the French Declaration of the Rights of Man and of the Citizen there is no mention of happiness, only of property. To the thrifty colonials the right to property made sense. Then why did Jefferson put the pursuit of happiness on a par with life and liberty?

It was no accident. Jefferson was a son of the eighteenth century and keenly interested in the Enlightenment that was so clearly visible in France. Burlamaqui, an obscure Italian-Swiss philosopher, had used the phrase in a close analysis of the reasons for the conjunction of life, liberty, and the pursuit of happiness. The necessity of Liberty is obvious; life might otherwise be spent in close confinement, but why Happiness? Burlamaqui defines it as the right to do these things which the individual finds worthy and enjoyable and consistent with the equal right of all other men. That made the triangle complete and universal.

Had Jefferson read Burlamaqui and borrowed the phrase? It is doubtful. The man's writings were little if at all known

in the colonies and few now know even his name. Probably
the versatile Virginian could read Italian a little, but not as
he read French and the classical languages. Possibly he knew
something of the man and his ideas through a French corre-
spondent, but even that is doubtful. It is more likely that
the minds of the two thinkers were in full accord and the
same terms came naturally to them both. The nature of such
things as life and liberty was much in the minds of eighteenth
century philosophers. That was the time when men were concerned to discover Man the universal.

The assertion that should have caused the most discussion
and criticism, the right of the people to alter or to abolish their
government whenever it becomes destructive of the rights
claimed, excited little interest. And yet here was the an-
nouncement of the right of revolution and the overthrow of
an existing regime in measured, matter-of-fact terms. This
was revolution stark and simple offered as part of the American
creed and little attention was paid to it. For most Americans the existing government was British and they were now
engaged in discarding it. The author of the Declaration was
clear-eyed and consistent. When Shays' Rebellion threatened
the government of Massachusetts ten years later he approved
it as infinitely preferable to tame acceptance of injustice.

The name of Thomas Jefferson is written in large letters
across our history. He was a graduate of William and Mary
College at Williamsburg, Virginia, the second oldest college
in America. As a student there he had formed a close friendship with three men who did more to educate him than the
struggling college. These men were George Wythe, probably
the best lawyer in the colonies, William Small, graduate of a
Scottish university and thoroughly trained in philosophy, and
Francis Fauquier, Lieutenant Governor of Virginia, an Oxford

product, student of the philosophy of law and of politics, cultured man of the world and inveterate gambler. This strangely assorted foursome dined often at the Raleigh Tavern in Williamsburg and the seventeen year old youth from the Piedmont added his share to the talk that spiced the meal.

The talents of the young man were many and varied. He played the violin; he was a better than fair architect and drew the plans for his monumental mansion on the high hill at Monticello; he was familiar with the scientists and scientific thought of his day; he was an accomplished linguist, a student and critic of Scripture, a horticulturist, and a master of political philosophy. To crown his achievements he founded the University of Virginia at Charlottesville and planned the curriculum, stressing science and modern languages, a revolutionary step in the educational program of the time. The epitaph which he composed for himself gives a glimpse of the man:

Author of the Declaration of Independence and of the statute for religious freedom in the state of Virginia and founder of the University of Virginia.

Those were the things for which he wished to be remembered. No mention is made of the fact that he had been a member of the Continental Congress, war-time governor of the state, minister to France, Secretary of State, Vice-President, and twice President of the United States.

This man was withdrawn and in spite of his wide writing revealed little of his inner self. He was involved in controversy all his life but he avoided the acrimony of debate and abhorred long speeches. It is possible that the clearest revelation of the inner man is to be found in the many long letters that he exchanged with crusty John Adams when in old age their many differences were forgotten and they wrote long letters to each other about religion, education, scientific change, and his hopes for his new university which he could see from his high hill of Monticello. It was a singular coincidence that these two men, once opponents, now friends, should have died on the same day, the fiftieth anniversary of the adoption of the Declaration of Independence.

Copies of the Declaration were printed as fast as the Philadelphia printers could run them off and distributed through the colonies, touching off noisy celebrations. In New York a cheering mob of soldiers and workmen pulled down the equestrian statue of George III which stood on the Battery at the lower end of Manhattan Island. When it was discovered that the statue was of lead some thrifty citizens set about the melting of this curious work of art and casting it into bullets to shoot the soldiers of the King. It is of record that the statue produced 42,500 bullets. It is not known how many of them found their mark.

While independence was being declared in Philadelphia the war in New England was marking time. Howe had sailed for Halifax and there were no British soldiers on the soil of Massachusetts. So far the middle and southern colonies had been able to view the war as something heard at a distance, almost in a foreign country, but their time was coming. Although New York was still far from being the largest city on the Continent it was a logical next step for the British if they were in earnest in their attempt to put down the rebellion. Situated at the mouth of the Hudson, a natural water highway to the north, New York stood on a narrow tongue of land between that river and the western entrance to Long Island Sound, another water highway to all of southern New England as well as to the length of fertile Long Island. The harbor had excellent anchorage for a large fleet and was well sheltered in all directions. The force that held this town might well have the middle colonies under control down as far as the

Chesapeake and with a little intelligent effort could isolate quarrelsome New England.

Added to the strategic potential of New York was the lukewarm interest of its citizens in the war. Many of the leading men were openly pro-British. The city had made smaller contribution to the Continental Army than any of the other important centers. Here the British could find ample fuel to fire their favorite hope of raising American regiments to fight under the British flag. It is quite possible that this town sent more men into the British army than into the American forces. Sir Henry Clinton, commander here through most of the war, could testify to the persistence of the British dream of setting Americans to fight Americans, thereby saving them money and time. Clinton's repeated appeals to London for more troops were usually met by the smug suggestion from Whitehall that he make use of the many local young men who were eager to don British uniforms and collect a little British gold.

Books have been written about the part played by those who rated their allegiance to the King above the cause of the colonials. The old practice was to call them Tories and stigmatize them as little better than traitors. Now we call them Loyalists and probably understand them better. No one quite knows how many there were of them. For a long time the British held to their wistful belief that the substantial property owning colonials were awaiting a chance to come over openly to the side of constitutional order, which of course was the King's side. The numbers undoubtedly varied with the colony, few in Massachusetts and Virginia, many in New York, northern New Jersey and eastern Pennsylvania. At least seventy thousand Loyalists left the country during the war, mostly for Canada, and probably more took the necessary oaths, paid their taxes, and kept their mouths shut.

To say that the Continental Army was composed of jail-birds, ignorant backwoodsmen, trouble makers, and general riffraff fails to take account of George Washington, Benjamin Franklin, John Adams, Nathanael Greene, Thomas Jefferson, and their kind. Loyalists who joined in actively with the British, as did the Johnsons and Butlers in the Mohawk Valley, ended by losing their land and sometimes their lives. The conduct of Johnson, Butler, and St. Leger in the Mohawk country, earned for them special detestation. It was Butler's Rangers and St. Leger's Loyal Greens who led the Iroquois to the infamous massacre at Wyoming in northeastern Pennsylvania, an act which is still remembered in that region. In the Carolinas and in Westchester County, New York, just north of the city, small bands of partisans claiming to represent one side or the other looted, burned, and killed, paying old grudges and creating new ones, benefiting neither side but adding greatly to the bitterness of feeling.

In spite of the constant appeals of British field commanders for more troops and the futile efforts to enlist Americans, the British forces available outnumbered the Americans in all the fighting with the exception of Saratoga and Yorktown. At the end of the war there were approximately 30,000 British troops in America; most of them in New York although they had lost some 10,000 at Saratoga and Yorktown. The Continental Army may have mustered 18,000 at its peak, but was usually far less. In the hard winter of 1777-1778 at Valley Forge it sank to five thousand or less, with no more than half fit for active duty. The men who stuck through that winter were the irreconcilables, the men who would never surrender.

The fightng around New York in the summer and fall of 1776 was disastrous for the patriot cause. This was Washington's first big test in major battle tactics and he was guilty of two blunders, either of which might have been fatal. He divided his army and sent the major part across the East River, apparently assuming that Howe would be as obliging as he had been at Bunker Hill. Then the battle positions he selected on the outskirts of what is now Brooklyn were exposed to flank attack and difficult to hold in any case. A contrary wind held the British ships in the lower bay and a heavy fog shielded the withdrawal to Manhattan Island when it became necessary for the Americans to pull back. Here the men from Gloucester, Marblehead, and Salem saved the American Army. For most of the night of August 28, John Glover's fishermen rowed boatloads of soldiers across to temporary safety, two miles to the round trip through blinding rain and then dense fog. There was no thrill or glory for these boatmen, only grim, tough, tight-lipped courage. It was said that the Commander in Chief was the last man to board the last boat. It had been a hard but a necessary lesson for him and one that he never forgot.

Such safety as the retreating army found on the Manhattan side was illusory. Ahead of them was still the long march up the narrow island with the enemy at their heels. Luck and General Howe's fondness for good food and drink helped the patriots a little. The comfortable home and well stocked cellar of Mrs. Murray was irresistible to the general and his staff and he promptly selected it as temporary field headquarters. There was no need for hurry. The rebels were on the run and a few more miles and hours would end the war. So — "Thank you, Mrs. Murray, another glass of that excellent Madeira." Mrs. Murray was a sincere Loyalist and meant well when she pressed more wine on Howe and his staff, but it was the retreating Continentals who had reason to thank her. After the war she went back to England where her son became a famous grammarian and a thorn in the flesh of generations of English schoolboys. Her hospitable home was on Murray

Hill near the present location of the Grand Central Station on Forty-second Street.

The wine and the polite talk at the Murray house gave the fast moving colonials time to reach Harlem Heights near the northern end of the island. In the deep depression that is now Harlem the American rear guard showed fight and set crack British troops back on their heels, giving their comrades a little more time and a little more distance — but not safety. They were still a long way from that, but in that deep hollow (then called the Hollow Way, now 125th Street, north of Columbia University) a picked body of Connecticut Rangers under Thomas Knowlton showed Scotch Highlanders that this ragged, hungry army could lash out viciously when the pursuers were too close on their heels. The British seemed on the verge of a rout, but Washington knew well what would be the cost of outright defeat and the loss of his own army. If that happened the war would end then and there. Whatever the odds he must keep his army alive.

Howe's combination of over-confidence and lethargy helped the Americans. It was not until well along in November that he could report the capture of Fort Washington at the upper end of the island and soon after of Fort Lee on the west bank of the Hudson. What is called the Battle of White Plains was not so much a single engagement as a series of small actions to cover the ferrying of Washington's army across to New Jersey.

Washington's objective was eastern Pennsylvania beyond the Delaware where he might rest and reorganize his badly beaten army; but urgent as was the need for speed the unpredictable General Charles Lee showed a strange reluctance to move his holding force from North Castle north of White Plains, even after the army was across the Hudson and waiting to press on toward the Delaware. Evidently his special talent was his ability to seek a decision as far as possible removed from the course chosen. Still he stood high with powerful men in Congress and Washington bore with him.

Once on the march Washington moved fast across New Jersey and into Pennsylvania, taking care not to leave any boats to lift the pursuers over the Delaware. Pennsylvania offered a respite from marching and rearguard fighting, but it was not to last long. The Continental Army was still an army in being, but the British held New York and most of New Jersey and proceeded to establish a line of posts running from Amboy near New York to Trenton, garrisoning them with small British and Hessian forces. Rall who had distinguished himself in the capture of Fort Washington was in command at Trenton. Back at headquarters in New York the amiable General Howe let it be known that an American winter was no time for active fighting and settled down for a comfortable hibernation.

British strength in the region had been considerably augmented by the arrival in New York of Admiral Sir Peter Parker's fleet and troopships bearing 2,500 soldiers under command of Sir Henry Clinton returning from a fruitless try at Charleston in South Carolina. Parker had taken his ten ships of the line into Charleston harbor expecting little trouble with the hastily constructed fort that guarded the entrance. The defense works were unimpressive, earthworks buttressed with palmetto logs, but the embankments and the soft palmetto absorbed the round shot from the ships, and the American gunners, commanded by Colonel William Moultrie, replied to such good purpose that the British drew off and headed for New York, arriving in time to enable Lord Cornwallis who was with Clinton to join in the pursuit of Washington. Cornwallis, having no memory of the near debacle of Bunker Hill, pressed the chase with vigor until the cautious Howe restrained him.

With fresh troops and a powerful fleet at his command Howe had good reason for satisfaction. Except for Boston and Charleston at opposite ends of the long coast line, the British were in control of the important ports. Philadelphia was near and could be taken by the mere stretching out of an arm. Washington, the "Old Fox," was hiding somewhere in Pennsylvania with his beaten and hungry army, which was reported to be melting away from sickness and desertion. The end of the rebellion was at hand, at least so said Howe. Washington thought otherwise, as events were soon to show.

Chapter V

Merry Christmas at Trenton

Washington's situation, on paper, was fully as desperate
as Howe depicted it. The daily attrition by sickness and desertion was not the only problem that the Americans faced.
The term of enlistment of many of them was expiring on December 31, and where would the army be then? Responding
to personal appeals for another six weeks of endurance enough
men agreed to stay on to enable Washington to plan a counter
stroke: nothing less than to cross the Delaware at night for a
surprise attack on Rall and his Hessians comfortably settled
at Trenton with every prospect of an easy winter. Time
pressed and the officers drove their men hard in preparation
for what was to come. Plans must be made, boats found or
built, boats' crews chosen, Massachusetts fishermen of course,
and orders issued. By superhuman efforts they were ready by
Christmas night of 1776. Even at that critical hour failure
threatened. Two smaller detachments under orders to cross
simultaneously lower down the river to take the Hessians in
the flank weakened at the sight of the flooded river and the
floating ice and decided that this was no night for a boatride.
The main body stood fast and set out with horses and Henry
Knox's cannon on board.

It was a bleak, stormy night with a high wind lashing

them with freezing sleet, but no storm was enough to stop the men of Marblehead when there was work to do. Emanuel Leutze's painting of Washington standing erect in the bow of the leading boat wrapped in his cloak and facing the storm is familiar to all Americans, but it is not generally known that the man who posed for Washington was Arnold Whitridge, a young American art student studying in Germany, the only man available who measured up to the dimensions of the Commander in Chief. (The art student's daughter heard her father tell the story and passed it along to this writer.) Nine hours were consumed in the crossing. The troops huddled in their thin clothing endured as soldiers must. As they marched to the attack through the driving sleet the only order that Washington, riding his chestnut sorrel in the lead, was heard to give was, "Press on! Press on, boys!"

In Trenton the Hessians were observing Christmas in proper German fashion. In the headquarters of Colonel Rall, their commander, were wine and cards and singing. Sentinels walked their posts in casual fashion or huddled in warm corners out of the wind. Even that crazy Washington would hardly venture an attack on such a night; but early dawn saw the Americans driving in on them. The fight was short and to the point. Out of the sixteen hundred Hessians a hundred were killed and eight to nine hundred were taken prisoner. Colonel Rall was among the dead. Washington had done it again.

The day before the crossing of the Delaware copies of Thomas Paine's pamphlet *Common Sense* were distributed among the troops as a call to action and a stimulant for the faint of heart. Paine was a stormy petrel of revolution. He was English born and early apprenticed to a maker of ladies' stays in Norwich, but his spirit rejected this servitude to the fashion of the day. His incendiary writing and speaking soon brought upon him the unfavorable attention of the authorities.

Threatened with a term in an English jail he fled to Philadelphia where he found employment as a hack writer for newspapers. His forceful style gained him readers, but he soon found the turning out of weekly articles on every conceivable theme only slightly less repellent than the making of of corsets for fashionable women.

Revolution against British tyranny was meat to his hungry soul and his *Common Sense*, which appeared six months before the Declaration of Independence, was a blistering indictment of governments in general and that of King George in particular. Nothing less than complete separation from England would satisfy him. "Society in every state is a blessing, but Government, even in its best state, is but a necessary evil; in its worst, an intolerable one. Government, like dress, is the badge of lost innocence; the palaces of kings are built upon the ruins of the bowers of paradise." The pamphlet was an instant success. Thousands of copies were printed and its effect on colonial minds was immeasurable. In the starving time at Valley Forge his *Crisis* with its trumpet call in the opening line, "These are the times that try men's souls," did much to stiffen the will to endure.

Paine's popularity declined with the end of the fighting. The wearisome details of governing did not concern him and as the fever of revolution rose in France he hastened to that country to lend a hand in overturning another monarchy. In Paris he landed in jail because of his criticism of the excesses of Robespierre and Danton in the Reign of Terror and he was in imminent danger of the guillotine when an appeal to the American Minister secured his release. Back to America he came bringing with him the key to the Bastille which he presented to Washington. That practical minded farmer eyed the cumbersome article, murmured "Ah, yes," and put it in his pocket. Where else would one put a key?

Paine's last pamphlet was *The Age of Reason,* an attack on organized religion and an appeal for free thinking, printed in 1794. An attack on Washington the following year was the last blow to his fame and he died in 1809 in obscurity and poverty. A hundred years later an American President, Theodore Roosevelt, denounced him as a "dirty little atheist." Whatever else he may have been, he was never that.

Ten days after the stunning surprise at Trenton, Washington was back in New Jersey, this time at Princeton, already a college town. Nassau Hall, which still stands on the Princeton campus, was British headquarters and strongly defended. Again the Americans staged a surprise, a flank movement at night. The campfires of the opposing forces were in sight of each other and the American fires were part of the deception. These were left burning with a small token party to give an appearance of an army preparing for battle the next morning. In the thick darkness the main body of the Continentals swung as quietly as possible by the flank, struck the British rear and sent it reeling in retreat. Nassau Hall was abandoned precipitately when Alexander Hamilton turned his cannon on it, and the way seemed open to the British supply base at New Brunswick. But the fast moving, hard hitting Cornwallis was coming at top speed from New York with fresh troops and the Continentals were near the end of their ammunition and their endurance and Washington knew it. Furthermore the extra time he had been granted was running out and he was in desperate need of rest and a chance to build up his army personnel again and gather fresh equipment and supplies. So he refused the temptation to make a push for the enemy's supply base and moved around the British right and headed for Morristown and winter quarters. When Cornwallis panted into the little town of Princeton he found only the litter of battle and the ashes of old fires.

Morristown, where Washington's long retreat may be said to have ended, is now a suburb of New York City in easy commuting distance, in sight of the high towers of Manhattan on clear days. In Revolutionary times it was a small country village planted on high ground with good supplies of water and fuel near at hand. The fighting men had used their extra time to good advantage. Broken and beaten as they had been in New York they had found somewhere the spirit to fight two successful engagements and take two thousand prisoners, convincing evidence of the ability of these ragged, hungry amateurs to hit back at their over-confident foe. After a weak and dangerous plan of battle on Long Island and Manhattan the Commander in Chief had shown high qualities of leadership and his army was still a force in being. The winter's rest was well earned.

With the British the energetic Cornwallis, baffled over his failure to catch the rebels at Princeton, put in for leave and sailed for England, leaving New York to Howe and Clinton. Both of these gentlemen were only too willing to sit the winter out in such comfort as the future metropolis offered, hoping that the war would wear itself out before spring came.

Chapter VI

Morristown to Valley Forge

In the two months that Washington spent at Morristown the war slumbered as far as any major movements were concerned. The officers of the Continentals spent their days rounding up recruits and whipping them into some kind of shape for fighting and marching. A siege of smallpox beset the camp and the problem of food was a daily one. In general the winter was about what might have been expected in the circumstances, not as bad as was to come. There were occasional mild forays, chiefly by the Americans. "Light Horse" Harry Lee, Virginia born, a graduate of Princeton, no kin to the British General Charles, struck a small British post at Paulus Hook, now Jersey City across the Hudson River from New York, and achieved at least a token success, which made no change in the slow progress of the war.

General Charles Lee appeared as Washington's second in command, a post that he owed to pressure from Congress. He was English born and claimed a considerable credit for his service with the British and more for his victorious career in Poland, about which there was little reliable information except that which he himself offered. His friends in Congress began to whisper behind their hands that he might be a better Commander in Chief than Washington. With such an experienced professional available why tolerate the blunderings of a colonel of Virginia militia?

There was one black mark against the name of Lee which should have given even a congressman something to think about. In the retreat he had dallied unnecessarily at North Castle, even ignoring peremptory orders to move out. He continued to hang back in the march across New Jersey and crowned his performance by carelessly allowing himself to be captured by a party of British skirmishers and then released with curious promptness. Much later it was learned that while a captive with the enemy he had given his captors information about Washington's plans, inaccurately as it happened. He also explained to his hosts how he thought the whole Continental Army including the commander could be scooped in. His suggestions to the Americans were equally extravagant. On one occasion in a staff meeting he proposed that the Continentals abandon the attempt to beat the unbeatable British on the seaboard and retire with such noncombatants as cared to go to the neighborhood of Pittsburgh and there lay the foundation of a new western empire.

Lee came to the end of his rope the next year at the battle of Monmouth. His rank entitled him to the command of the advance corps, but when it was offered him he rejected it scornfully as unworthy of his standing. Lafayette was next in line and accepted promptly with Anthony Wayne as his able second. When Lee learned that this post was the most important in the contemplated action, as well as by far the largest he promptly changed his mind and clamored for it as his right. Lafayette gave way at once. When the battle was joined Lee as usual was evasive and vague in his battle orders and ended by giving none at all. In spite of bad leadership the Americans went forward effectively and the outcome seemed certain when Lee, mysterious as always, ordered a general withdrawal. The result of course was dismay and confusion. At that critical moment Washington appeared, ordered Lee to the rear and took command in person.

What did Washington say to Lee when he ordered him to the rear? A witness to the meeting reported later that Washington "swore like an angel from heaven," however that is. Mercy Warren of Plymouth, who wrote a history of the Revolution about fifteen years later, refers delicately to some "warm expressions" used by Washington. They were at least that. As for Lee, he was tried by court-martial and suspended from the army for a year, which turned out to be permanent. He retired to a log cabin on a small estate in Virginia where he lived out his days with only his dogs as companions. He was in no way related to the Lees of Virginia, as his conduct abundantly proved.

It might be noted that in the battle of Monmouth a force of seven hundred negroes fought with the Americans and gave a good account of themselves.

The fate of Lee at Monmouth has been an anticipation. Monmouth was in late June of 1778, but for Washington at Morristown it was still the spring of 1777. He had chosen Morristown partly because it gave him a better point from which to keep an eye on the movements of General Howe in New York. It was certain that Howe would move, but in which direction? Would it be up the Hudson to cut the line of communication and supply with New England or south to threaten Philadelphia? When they knew the answer to this question the Americans could move with speed to check him. To Washington's surprise Howe's decision was for Philadelphia by way of Chesapeake Bay in spite of the delay caused by the longer sea voyage. Why not up the Delaware, a much shorter route? A possible answer was Howe's overestimate of the strength of the American batteries on the lower Delaware. How much, if anything, did Howe know of a movement down from Canada that Germain was planning with Burgoyne to command it? Here is a first class mystery to which no one quite holds the key. Perhaps Howe rashly calculated that he could take Philadelphia easily and still do whatever was necessary in aid of Burgoyne.

As soon as he had reliable intelligence of Howe's plan Washington led his reinforced and rested army south through peaceful, prosperous Bucks County in Pennsylvania to the defense of Philadelphia. From Elkton at the head of Chesapeake Bay to Philadelphia it is only slightly over fifty miles, today at least. Perhaps it was longer in 1777. The British made it in thirty days. Washington met them at Chad's Ford on the Brandywine, a small river midway. Faulty intelligence misled the Americans as to the point of the British main attack and Howe skilfully turned the defenders' flank. Even so the fight at the ford was a hot one which the British won with a loss of six hundred against the Americans' thousand. it was September 26, 1777, when Howe entered Philadelphia. There was a brisk fight at Germantown, now a fashionable suburb of Philadelphia, which the Americans lost, at least partly due to an undue regard for standard battle theory. Several of the British had taken post in a large stone mansion belonging to Benjamin Chew. Standard theory taught that a fortified position should never be bypassed, so precious time was wasted in a useless task. The joining of the three attacking columns went hopelessly astray to reduce a post that was of little value when it was taken now that Howe was safely ensconced in the capital city. When he heard the news Benjamin Franklin in Paris remarked, "Say rather Philadelphia has taken Howe." It turned out that way.

After the departure of Howe, Sir Henry Clinton was in command in New York, where the British were making themselves quite comfortable, some of them profitably so.   Four quartermasters took their turn at the official purse, each one resigning when his private accumulations had reached a satisfactory size.   In eighteenth century England the fiscal conscience of public men was an elastic article.   Appointments, promotions, and perquisites were bought and sold, if not in the open market at least without shame or hesitation.   Even the elder Pitt, the great Lord Chatham, was not above the use of bribery to gain his ends; and Lord North, George III's favorite minister of state, had no trouble in combining public corruption with scrupulous honesty in his private affairs. Charles James Fox, staunch friend of the colonies, became a member of the House of Commons at the ripe age of twenty — an honor that could hardly have been earned by proven political merit at that age.

In the midst of the turmoil of war and capture and campaign, Sir Henry Clinton was in command in New York and destined to hold his post there until the end of the war.   Whatever the feelings of his officers Sir Henry was an unhappy man. Fat and bad-tempered he was overwhelmed by the flood of Loyalist refugees that poured in on him as the war swirled around him.   All of them demanded living quarters, and most of the able-bodied men among them clamored for places and titles appropriate to their imagined deserts.   It was in vain that Clinton besought the government to send him more troops and annually offered his resignation.   The government's reply was to urge him to organize Loyalist regiments with which the rebellion might easily be squelched.   British faith in the existence of a large reservoir of loyalty needing only to be tapped died hard.   At that Clinton did not do so badly.   By August 1778, he had filled two such regiments and thirteen

more were in the making, or so he thought. While his actual
military contributions were slight, Clinton did keep a kind of
order in New York and he provided a haven for the Loyalists
who were there because they had nowhere else to go.

The winter of 1777-8 was a gay one for Howe and his
men in Philadelphia. The citizens were ostensibly friendly
and many of them hospitable. The young officers danced
well and dined agreeably in comfortable homes. The soldiers
were well housed and the food was usually abundant. Clothing was warm, including woolen nightcaps that were issued
to some of them. While they rested and feasted less than thirty
miles away the Continentals, now reduced to five thousand,
less than half of whom were fit for action, spent the winter at
Valley Forge. Even the sturdiest were cold and hungry most
of the time. On paper a regiment of disciplined troops could
have rounded up the whole army at Valley Forge in two or
three days of marching and fighting. Why didn't they try it?

The solution to this puzzle is probably to be found in the
commander himself. Both of the brothers Howe thought well
of themselves as conciliators as well as fighters, combined roles
that are difficult to play. Both felt themselves to be genuinely
friendly to the colonists, as had been their older brother who
had fought beside colonial militia in the Seven Years War.
After that war was over the militiamen of Massachusetts built
a monument to his memory on the field where he had died.
Both Howes were sure that the Americans were only waiting
for the chance to come back to the old relationship of cherish-
ing mother and obedient daughter, and care must be taken
to avoid discouraging such a step. The names of some of the
ships in the convoy that brought Howe's army from Halifax
to New York are thought-provoking: *Felicity, Three Sisters,
Amity's Admonition, Good Intent, Friendship, Father's Good
Will.*

Entries in the journal of Ambrose Serle, civilian secretary to Lord Howe, the admiral, reveal the anomalous position of his chief, as well as the diarist's own British Tory attitude. On July 12, 1776, Serle records: "We also heard that the colonists had now announced the colonies to be independent States, with several other articles of intelligence that proclaim the villainy and the madness of these deluded people." There are frequent references to the wretched state of the Continental troops about to disband in disgust. The American soldiers are described as worthless jailbirds, loafers, deserters from the British Army, not the sort of people one could associate with at all. American democracy was an absurdity, illustrated by the sight of Governor Trumbull of Connecticut waiting his turn in a "common Barber Shop," something that could hardly be found in a self-respecting society.

In leisure moments Serle occupied himself with outlining a possible constitution for such inferior people. It was to have a parliament of sorts coordinate with that at Westminster, if they would accept the British system of an hereditary nobility, "in order to counteract all levelling ideas." Other Englishmen seriously considered such a possibility, possibly including Lord Howe, finding nothing absurd in the thought of the Duke of Mount Vernon or Earl Adams of Braintree. Serle really boils over with indignation when a letter addressed to George Washington, Esq., is refused at the American headquarters on the ground that no such person was known there. "So high is the vanity and the Insolence of these Men! The Truth is the Punctilio of an address would never have retarded the Reception of a Letter from a Person, with whose high Rank and Commission they were well acquainted, and whose Bravery and Honor are well known everywhere; if their minds had been in the least disposed to the Duties of Humanity, Law, and Allegiance." A second letter addressed to "George Washington, etc., etc., etc." met the same fate except that it came to the attention of Washington himself, who remarked drily: "It is true the *et ceteras* imply everything, but it is no less true that they imply anything."

On May 8th, 1778, Serle comments on the news "that France had been base enough to conclude a Treaty of commerce with our profligate and abandoned Rebels," — and that in consequence a War with that Power, and therefore with Spain was inevitable. "May the God of Hosts be with us, and He, who governs battles our refuge! Surely the righteous One will not prosper the Iniquity of our Enemies, nor suffer a cause, founded in Falsehood, Baseness, and Rebellion to succeed. The Judge of the whole Earth will do right." Nowhere is there a hint that the God of battles might be contemplating the defeat of the British.

In Philadelphia General Howe and his army settled down for a pleasant winter. A few miles away the Continentals starved and froze and worked. Von Steuben, the Prussian drill master, spent his days in much needed training in the arts of the soldier. In spite of hardship and the inevitable grumbling of the soldiers it was not a wasted winter. Food was scarce of course, but the Americans were skillful foragers and often helped themselves to the loaded wagons coming in from the countryside with food for the British. Allan McLane was one of the best of these military highwaymen, sometimes cutting off convoys in view of British sentinels. But for this the Americans would have been even hungrier.

Grim as it was, there were lighter moments even at Valley Forge. General Howe's spaniel strayed into the American lines bearing his master's name on his collar. He was promptly returned to the British under a flag of truce. His grateful owner wrote an appropriate note of thanks to the American commander. Presumably the wanderer was duly restricted to his quarters under charges of being Absent Without Leave.

The privates and noncoms were housed in huts fourteen by sixteen feet in area, six and a half feet high, with one door and one window. Twelve men were expected to sleep in such quarters, of course without heat or sanitary provision. Of the food, Washington reported that his men ate every kind of horse food except hay. Bread, if any, was made out of a bizarre mixture of wheat, buckwheat, rye, and Indian corn, in such proportions as the supply permitted. Quarters for officers were slightly larger but no more comfortable. Washington and his staff occupied the house of Isaac Potts. In spite of the wretched living conditions Mrs. Washington spent most of the winter with her husband, as she had done at Cambridge and Morristown.

Howe's hope that the rebellion would collapse automatically with the capture of the chief city proved another airy illusion. The only political result was that Congress decamped hastily to York, Pennsylvania, and resumed their sessions. At this time of crisis the Continental Congress was not a pretty spectacle. Not content with their failure to provide an adequate commissary, some of the members continued to plot the displacement of Washington. The Conway Cabal, as it was called, involved General Horatio Gates, who was succeeding Charles Lee as a favorite of Congress. The plotters even tried to interest the young Lafayette and outlined to him their plan for an invasion of Canada with Conway second in command to Lafayette who was to lead it. The bait was offered at a dinner in York. Lafayette heard the plotters through and then proposed a toast, "To the Commander in Chief of the Armies of the United States!" No more was heard of an expedition to Canada and when an incriminating letter from Conway to Gates fell into Washington's hands Conway wrote a sniveling letter of apology and resignation to the commander and presently slipped away to France.

Thomas Conway was Irish-born but was taken to France at the age of six and as a young man served in the French Army. When Silas Deane appeared in Paris in the role of an assistant to Franklin he soon became known as the source of recommendations for French officers wishing to serve, with high rank and pay, in America. Conway had no trouble wangling a letter to Congress in his behalf and Congress obligingly made him a brigadier general and later major general over the opposition of Washington who was being embarrassed by the flood of gentlemen adventurers with outstretched hands. After his exposure and return to France he served with the French in India. When revolution came to France, perhaps mindful of his bad luck in America, this weathervane chose the royalist side and died in exile.

Gates, it must be said, was no such dubious character as Conway. As a captain in the British Army he had marched with Braddock to the tragic defeat in the attack on Fort Duquesne, where he was wounded. America drew him back after the Seven Years War and in 1772 he became a plantation owner in Virginia. In spite of his poor performance as Commander in Chief in the Carolinas he had a good record as an administrator, a rare specimen in the Continental Army. When the war was over he returned to his Virginia land, but his deep dislike of slavery led him to sell his Virginia holdings and move to a farm which he called Rose Hill on Manhattan Island, near what is now a crowded tenement area at Twenty-third Street and Second Avenue. There he died.

In Philadelphia the social season came to its climax in a grand water pageant planned and directed by the doomed John André, the most brilliant and popular of the younger British officers. A special supper room was built for the spectacle two hundred and ten feet long and forty feet in height. One of the Philadelphia homes where André had been a welcome guest was that of the Shippen family, ostensibly favorable to the patriot cause but friendly to the British. There was a charming, lively young daughter Peggy. André asked her to take a leading part in his *Mischianza*, as he called his show. This was too outright to suit her hesitant father. Fortunately he had an ostensible reason for declining; the young ladies among the performers were expected to wear Turkish costumes with baggy trousers, of course quite unsuited for modest young ladies, and Miss Peggy was not even a guest. The sole reason for recalling this trifling incident is that she was soon to become Mrs. Benedict Arnold and a controversial figure in another drama, this time a tragedy.

André's *Mischianza* marked the end of the British stay in Philadephia. Howe returned to England, having accomplished nothing much, and Clinton came down from New York to take his place. It had been a pleasant winter but a wasted one. Franklin's shrewd prophecy had been fulfilled. For once Clinton made a prompt decision and acted on it. He would evacuate Philadelphia and take the troops back to New York. To move the army by sea was slow, cumbersome, and dangerous with the possibility of a French fleet off the mouth of the Delaware. He would march his men across New Jersey and send the baggage and the unhappy Tories and their families by ship. At Valley Forge an arch bearing Washington's words marks the site of that starvation camp:

> Naked and starving as they are we cannot enough admire the incomparable patience and fidelity of the soldiery.

It is mildly amusing now, a hundred and eighty years later, to note that as Clinton was evacuating Philadelphia a ship from England brought in a special commission charged with the duty of making terms with the stubborn rebels. The head was the Earl of Carlisle, an honest man but a bewildered one. The other members were William Eden and George Johnstone, one time governor of Florida, now regarded by the British as an authority on America and Americans. The only thing wrong with this commission which the King had grudgingly approved was that they had nothing to offer beyond the vague assurance that if the Americans would lay down their arms and take an oath of allegiance to King and Parliament all would be forgiven, they hoped.

Johnstone's contribution to the negotiations was an attempt to bribe Joseph Reed, an important member of Congress, by offering him ten thousand pounds sterling. It was reported that Reed rather stuffily replied: "I am not worth the purchasing, but such as I am the King of England is not rich enough to buy me." Alexander Wedderburn, the King's Solicitor General, accurately described Johnstone as an offensive bungler. My Lord Carlisle reported that American mosquitoes were as big as sparrows and sailed sadly back to England taking with him an American raccoon.

Clinton's long march from Philadelphia to Sandy Hook, where ships would be waiting to carry the soldiers up the bay to New York, offered tempting opportunity for attack. An army strung out in line of march is particularly vulnerable even with British grenadiers guarding the rear. The capture of Burgoyne had removed the menace from the north and the Continentals who had fought at Saratoga could now be added to Washington's force. Staff discussions were long and sometimes acrimonious. Hot tempered Wayne called for immediate action and others backed him up. Charles Lee as usual dragged his feet. It was not possible for American troops to beat seasoned British veterans. The gallant Lafayette of course thirsted for action. Finally the decision was taken, but time had been lost and the British were moving fast. Here the impossible Lee argued and delayed, refusing command of the main spearhead, then demanding it as has been told. In the battle of Monmouth the British rear guard was on the verge of being folded up when Lee ordered a withdrawal. That was the end of Lee, but he had succeeded in turning what promised to be a smashing victory into a draw.

Win or lose the Battle of Monmouth was the last major action of the Revolution to be fought in the North.

CHAPTER VII

Through the Wilderness to Saratoga

While Washington sparred with Howe around Philadelphia and then settled down for a winter of watchful waiting and freezing at Valley Forge danger threatened from Canada. Take a look at a map of New York and the region north of it. The Hudson River was wide and deep with tides all the way to Albany and beyond, a tempting highway as the Dutch had learned nearly a century and a half earlier. If an enemy force held that river it meant the isolation of New England and the end of reinforcements and supplies from that direction. So the Secretary of State for the Colonies, Lord George Germain, must have reasoned. Germain was one of the chief figures in the official game of directing the war from a commodious desk in London. His chief qualifications for the task were complete self-confidence and a sublime effrontery that had brought him through a charge of cowardice and a court martial for his conduct at the battle of Minden.

Lord George's plan was simple in concept and disastrous in execution. He studied the map and dreamed up a great scissors movement, with a British force coming down from Canada along the route of the French and Indian raids in the old days before the French had lost Canada on the Heights of Abraham. Somewhere about Albany this force would meet another British army that Howe would lead up the Hudson from New York. Thus would the map be neatly cut. Fortunately for the colonials Germain was possesed of a large stock of blissful ignorance of the difficulties attendant on moving an army cumbered with artillery and a long wagon train through the tangled wilderness of the Adirondacks. The French and Indians had done it more than once; why shouldn't the British do it now? They did, but not in Indian fashion, and at a heavy cost in time and exhaustion. In addition to his baggage train Burgoyne dragged with him more than a hundred pieces of artillery including several huge twenty-four pounders for the reduction of American fortifications on the way. Incidentally there were no fortifications nearer than West Point, but the heavy guns lumbered along through the wilderness.

Before he sailed from London to take command of the northern invasion Lord John Burgoyne, "Gentleman Johnny," made a bet of fifty guineas with Charles James Fox that he would be back in London victorious by Christmas and the war would be over. He loved to gamble and this was probably his biggest bet. How much did he know of Germain's plan or of Howe's alteration of it? It is almost certain that he knew the plan; this was proved by his own treatise *Thoughts for Conducting the War from the Side of Canada,* approved by authority. When he reached Quebec early in May 1777, Carleton, the commander there, had told him of a letter from Howe referring vaguely to that general's own designs on Philadelphia. Burgoyne seems to have dismissed this lightly as a mild variation of the grand scheme. His own orders were to proceed to Albany and he set to work.

There is a tale of a further mixup in London of which

Burgoyne probably knew nothing. According to this somewhat apocryphal legend the plans were drawn and placed before Germain in London, but some of the details were in rough draft and the Secretary was a stickler in matters of form and demanded a "fair copy" for his distinguished signature. Besides he was due for a pleasant weekend at a great country house. So the orders were pushed aside while he went off for his breath of country air. The ship that was to have carried them to Howe sailed with the tide and there was to be no other sailing for a fortnight. The story may not be true, but it serves to illustrate the haphazard character of British strategy in this bewildering American war.

A large part of the force at Burgoyne's disposal was made up of Germans rented from petty German rulers. Hessians fought well with Howe in the fighting around New York and Hessians held the post at Trenton where Washington caught them the day after Christmas; now more than twenty-five hundred were to have a taste of frontier warfare. The use of Germans in a British army had a simple reason. King George had found himself in difficulty securing enough troops for his war in America. The average Englishman hated service in the army or navy and the specimens that the press gangs were able to pick up were not too promising. The pay was small, the food often poor, and the discipline cruel. George turned first to Russia, but the Empress Catherine refused to be interested and offered the biting comment that the hiring of foreign soldiers to be used in a war with his own colonists was beneath the dignity of a king, meaning George III. Some of the smaller German states were not so considerate of the royal feelings. Furthermore here was a chance for them to turn an honest penny and treaties were agreed upon by which nearly twenty thousand German lads were to be turned over to the dubious mercies of the British. Approximately seventeen thousand were actually delivered, nearly three thousand of them marching with Burgoyne.

George Otto Trevelyan in his excellent *History of the American Revolution* describes the marching equipment of the Hessians: a high cap with a heavy brass plate on the front, a long coat, a canteen holding a gallon, and a huge sword, "that had never killed anything except the calf or pig of a Loyalist farmer." To this may be added for the horseless Brunswicker Dragoons twelve-pound boots plus heavy spurs. One can imagine the derision of the men in buckskin, stepping softly in moccasins at the swift pace set by Ethan Allen and Daniel Morgan.

One example of the terms of rental is given in the treaty made by the British with the Duke of Brunswick calling for an overall payment of between fifty-five and sixty thousand pounds sterling for two years service, plus payment of thirty crowns per head for those killed, three wounded to be counted as one dead. Loot, presumably, was the personal perquisite of the looter.

The Brunswickers with Burgoyne were commanded by Baron von Riedesel who took with him as to a family picnic the Baroness and their three young daughters. This was fortunate for the historian as the Baroness's *Letters and Journals Relating to the War of the American Revolution and the Capture of the German Troops at Saratoga* sheds much light on this ill-starred adventure. Burgoyne she regarded as a brave general with bad habits. "He spent half the nights in singing and drinking and amusing himself with the wife of a commissary who was his mistress and who, as well as he, loved champagne." It should be noted that thirty of the wagons in the baggage train were reserved for the general's personal paraphernalia, apparently largely uniforms and champagne. The Riedesels were not the only family party with Burgoyne's army. In all seventy-seven of the Brunswickers were accompanied by their wives.

This invasion force set forth from the neighborhood of Crown Point near the northern end of Lake Champlain early in July of 1777, headed for Fort Ticonderoga at the other end of the lake. This post, taken so easily by Vermont and Massachusetts militia early in the war, had been called the Gibraltar of America, but it was really in bad repair and scantily garrisioned. The commander was Arthur St. Clair, formerly an officer in the British Army, fortunately both brave and intelligent. When he discovered that the British were dragging cannon to the top of a high hill commanding the interior of the fort he and his men promptly decamped.

That was the last of the easy days for Burgoyne. From there on the route led through a tangled wilderness of fallen trees, swamp, and streams that must be forded. It was early July and the weather was hot and sticky and swarms of mosquitoes made life a torment for the marching men. At the northern end of Lake George there was a choice of routes, by water down the lake or by a road that must be cut the length of the lake through a tangle that grew worse rather than better. In spite of the obvious advantages of the water route Burgoyne chose the land; after all it was only twenty miles and then they hoped to find more open country with occasional farms and villages. And not far beyond was Albany — their destination and the place where they would end the war.

The pace from the head of Champlain had been slow enough, but it was rapid transit to what lay ahead of them. Colonial axemen had been busy felling trees to add to the deadfalls and windfalls that already barred the way. Bridges strong enough to bear the weight of the artillery and the loaded wagons must be built as streams grew deeper. Between bridge-building and the laying of corduroy road the pace slowed to a crawl, sometimes less than half a mile a day. It was only twenty miles, but it cost the British twenty-six precious days.

A constant problem with Burgoyne was the control of his Indian allies. The use of Indians as scouts and skirmishers had been part of Germain's grand plan, a logical adjunct to his dream of masses of Tory regiments fighting for their King. Some of the eastern Iroquois came and Burgoyne made them a speech warning them that their white brothers did not scalp the dead or torture captives and that they must fight the white man's way. This was sheer nonsense to the Indians and some of them left in disgust. Enough stayed to embarrass the British. A ghastly tragedy highlighted the problem. A Miss Janet McCrae, the fiancee of a Tory officer with the British, was on the way to join her lover to be married and foolishly trusted to half a dozen Mohawks as guides and guards. Soon after, one of the Indians appeared with a scalp easily identified by length and color as that of Janet McCrae. Burgoyne's threat of punishment was incomprehensible to the Indians. This was war and a scalp was a scalp, a badge of honor in the tribe, and more Indians faded into the forest. The story was told and retold and more recruits appeared for the Continentals.

Burgoyne had great need of horses for the guns and wagons and, if possible, mounts for the dragoons with Riedesel. Also there was always need for more powder. When word came of militia with horses and ammunition gathering near the small town of Bennington in Vermont, he ordered the Baron to send a force to seize the supplies and scatter the militia, and of course to assemble as many as possible of the local Loyalists who were always expected. Baum was to command the raiders with orders to move fast and take the rebels by surprise. Another force under the command of an officer named Breyman was sent off a day or two later to cooperate

with Baum and if necessary support him. Baum and Breyman hated each other and could be counted on to cooperate
accordingly. In fact the supporting force never reached Bennington.

The surprise that Burgoyne hoped for backfired of course.
Stark and Allen waiting at Bennington with their grim fighters
knew more about the movements of the Germans than the Germans themselves knew. John Stark was one of the unpredict-
ables on the American side, unbeatable on his good days, but
not all his days were good. Most of all he resented a Continental Army and swore that anyone of his men from the New
Hampshire Grants was a match for half a dozen of the Continentals. His hot temper was often more powerful than his
judgment. At Bennington he was to have one of his good
days. Along with Allen and Stark and their men there were
militia from the Berkshires in Massachusetts, equally tough
fighters and good marksmen. They had brought their clergyman with them, the Reverend Thomas Allen of Pittsfield, who
marched with his congregation into battle when the time came.

It had been raining heavily but there were signs of clearing and the night before the fight the reverend gentleman
urged Stark to attack the next day rain or shine. His men had
come up to fight and not to wait about for better weather.
Stark made curt answer: "As soon as the Lord shall once more
send us sunshine, if I don't give you fighting enough I'll never
ask you to come out again!" The weather cleared and in the
morning Stark spoke again. Pointing at the advancing enemy
he called to his men: "Ours before night or Molly Stark's a
widow."

It was a hard fight lasting most of the day, but at the end
of it two hundred and seventeen of the thousand Hessians were
casualties and the rest were prisoners. Of the Americans fourteen were killed and forty-two wounded. In terms of numbers

involved it was a minor engagement, but it was a bad omen for the invaders, although Burgoyne tried to make light of it.

There was still another complication in the plan that had seemed so simple to Lord Germain three thousand miles away. Not only was Howe to move up the Hudson from New York, but Barry St. Leger, a lieutenant colonel with a good reputation for coolheadedness in action, was to move down from the post at Oswego on Lake Ontario with a mixed force of troops and Indians, capture Fort Stanwix, and march down the Mohawk River to join in the grand finale somewhere about Albany. Now there was bad news about St. Leger. Fort Stanwix had proved more stubborn than had been expected and refused to yield. The local militia, mostly from Tryon County, who had reason to hate Tories as much as Indians, were caught in an ambush at Oriskany and took heavy losses which included their leader Nicholas Herkimer, one of the German settlers, who had himself propped against a tree so that he might the better rally and direct his neighbors.

Benedict Arnold, a man of mystery at this time, was somewhere to the eastward with a reputedly large force of Continentals coming fast to the aid of the beleaguered settlers. Rumors, largely fomented by Arnold, magnified the numbers that were on the way, and the Indians, who had no taste for a siege under any circumstances and were glutted with the slaughter at Oriskany, disappeared and St. Leger was forced back to Oswego with the wearied remnants of his command. Burgoyne may have clung to his belief that Howe at least would not fail him, but about this time Howe was fighting his slow way up from the head of Chesapeake Bay toward his coveted goal of Philadelphia. Burgoyne at least was following his orders as well as he could. Go to Albany! That much at least was clear.

It was at sturdy Fort Stanwix that the Stars and Stripes

were first flown in battle. The story of Betsy Ross as the "maker" of the first American flag is a gallant gesture as the record shows. The flag unfurled to the April breeeze at Concord was probably the Massachusetts provincial flag, showing an arm holding a sword, now used on the official crest of the state. Washington's flag at Cambridge was a forerunner of the stars and stripes, with the crosses of St. George and St. Andrew where the stars now appear. There was one stripe for each colony. It was Francis Hopkinson of Philadelphia, a signer of the Declaration of Independence, who designed the present flag. At most the useful Betsy stitched the first official flag according to Hopkinson's design. The one flown at Fort Stanwix was hastily put together for the occasion, the blue cut from a soldier's jacket and the red from a woman's petticoat — not Betsy's.

When news came of St. Leger's retreat from Fort Stanwix even the buoyant Burgoyne might well have had his moments of despair. Of course there was still the chance of help from the south, Clinton if not Howe could hardly fail him at this climax in the long effort. After all he had thanked the footless Breyman for his attempt to cooperate with Baum at Bennington, calling it a very pretty little success, surely a record in optimism. About this time he received a vague note from Sir Henry Clinton in New York offering to send a force of two thousand men to reduce the loosely held rebel forts, Stony Point and Montgomery, to ease the pressure on Burgoyne. Those posts were a long way from Albany, but Clinton did take them — and then ordered his "reinforcements" back to New York.

Burgoyne's army was wasting and time was running out. By this time Horatio Gates had arrived at Albany to take command of the American defense, superseding Philip Schuyler, the Hudson Valley aristocrat and staunch patriot. Reinforcements were gathering for the Americans, militia from Massachusetts and Connecticut, groups and small companies from the New York countryside. Gates's army was growing and Burgoyne's shrinking. If the invaders were ever to reach Albany they must strike now or be overwhelmed. The first day of battle was September 19. A three-pronged advance of British and Germans encountered the Americans at Freeman's Farm, an abandoned group of small clearings surrounded by belts of woodland a few miles south of the present town of Saratoga.

It was here that they first saw the American rifleman. Daniel Morgan and his mountaineers from Virginia came though the trees with their long rifles and began to pick off officers at ranges beyond the reach of muskets. There were not many of them but as sharpshooters they were annoying and the weird gobbling of their turkey call was disturbing. The Germans had riflemen too, *Jaegers*, men who had been hunters and foresters at home. They were good shots and fast marchers, but the continental manual of arms handcuffed them with its slow motion and the practice of firing by volleys. These strange Americans loaded and fired at will.

The outcome of the fighting that day was indecisive and the British losses were more than they could afford, but Burgoyne praised his men for their victorious conduct. He could hardly know or believe that this wilderness farm was the nearest he was to come in his effort to reach Albany. On October 7 he struck again on practically the same ground, although the military geographers call this the battle of Bemis Heights. Gates was seeking to avoid general action, hoping to win by wearing down the British with his superior numbers. It was the fiery, ubiquitous Arnold who turned what Gates hoped would be only a defensive maneuver into a smashing victory. Arnold was still a mystery; without command he appeared suddenly with the Massachusetts militia and drove a deep wedge into Burgoyne's line. At the climax of the battle Arnold was wounded in the leg, the same leg that had stopped a bullet at Quebec, but he had turned the tide. If he had died then his fame would have been secure. On the battlefield there is a monument to "the most brilliant soldier of the Continental Army." No name is given, but there in eight words is the tragedy of Benedict Arnold.

Burgoyne had a faint hope of withdrawing to the ruins of Ticonderoga, but it was of brief duration and on October 17, 1777, he surrendered. Colonel Baldwin of the Massachusetts militia recorded the closing act in his journal: "About 11 o'clock A.M., the enemy laid down there arms and marched thro our army the most agreeable sight that ever my eyes beheld. Burgoin's army that capitulated there were 6,000 and of them 2,448 were British."

The faithful little Baroness recorded her agreeable surprise, as she passed in her caleche through the Americans, at the immobile silence of these rude, crude backwoods warriors as the losers passed through their lines. Gates had asked that they bear themselves as become the victors, but it is to be written down to the credit of the men that there were no hoots or jeers as the sullen or stolid losers marched past. For once at least these men were soldiers. The Baroness and her three daughters were taken under the hospitable wing of Philip Schuyler in his own home and her record of the campaign ended on a pleasant note.

Of General Gates the report is confusing, to say the least. When the fighting was done with he showed great leniency, inviting the beaten Burgoyne to dinner and drinking a toast to King George in return to the loser's toast to General Washington. Then he followed through by permitting Burgoyne to write the terms of surrender, even styling the document a

Convention, presumably a less humiliating label than Surrender. But viewed as a whole Gates's behavior was not greatly to his credit. Not only did he give the wounded Arnold an extremely cold shoulder, understandable for an orthodox commander dealing with that stormy, uncontrollable figure, but he delayed unaccountably in reporting the outcome officially. When he did deign to send in his report it was addressed to the Continental Congress, rather than to his official superior General Washington. That long-suffering leader refused to take offense at such a flagrant breach of proper procedure, contenting himself with a mild expression of regret that he had been forced to rely on rumor and unofficial sources for his information.

By the terms of the "Convention" the captured army was marched to Boston where it was to wait until ships could be provided to carry them back to England. Burgoyne sailed on the first boat available in order to set about defendng himself against the inevitable attacks. The loss of an army of six thousand with arms, artillery, and supplies was a bitter pill for Parliament and the cabinet, but the King persisted in his refusal to consider anything but the crushing of the rebellion.

Congress proved less lenient than Gates had been. Naturally ships for six thousand men were not easy to find so there was delay. Congress dallied and debated. Gates had exceeded his authority in promising passage to England. What reason was there for thinking that the troops, once back in England, would not be reorganized and sent back to fight again under a different leader to better purpose? In the end nothing was done. After a tiresome stay in Boston they were marched to Virginia and turned loose in the Piedmont and the Shenandoah Valley. There they settled, the Germans perhaps merging with other Germans drifting down from Pennsylvania, others no doubt filtering back across the Atlantic to their respective homelands after peace was made. They were merely part of the inevitable flotsam of war.

Of Burgoyne little needs to be said. He had trusted too much to the Germain plan and to his own *Thoughts for Conducting the War from the Side of Canada.* He had carried with him too many flamboyant uniforms and too many cases of champagne; he had laughed too much and wasted too much time in gentle dalliance with the wife of the commissary officer who was also fond of laughing and drinking. But with all his faults he alone had his eyes fixed on the goal at Albany. He had shown heroism of a kind and his personal courage was without blemish.

The repercussions of his surrender were large and immediate, fresh hope for Washington and the men who followed him and more troops for the "ragged Continentals." Most of all, here was the needed evidence for the hesitant Vergennes in Paris that the American cause justified support. It was not yet as clear as it would be soon that here was the turning of the tide. There were still hard days ahead with defeats and frustrations and postponements, but to us today the road runs from Saratoga to Yorktown.

CHAPTER VIII

A Hero Turns Traitor

In comparison with the grim winter at Valley Forge the spring of 1778 should have been bright with hope for the Americans. The dangerous threat down the Hudson River had been beaten off and the enemy had lost an army and a major general. Howe had gone back to England, for good, and the lethargic Clinton had accomplished the evacuation of Philadelphia. The British still held New York and Newport, nothing more. To crown the good news the treaty of alliance with France had been signed.

But there was a reverse side to the shield. The army that had been in Philadelphia was now in New York. Perhaps Clinton might decide now to make the thrust up river that Howe had avoided or postponed. If he did his advantage in manpower and material would put the unfinished fortifications at West Point in serious danger. Even the French alliance had its drawbacks. How soon could our new partner come to our aid and with what material? The British still held the seas, and taking a French army in convoy from France to America was not an attractive idea. Aid from France was not a new thing. Well before, that able, crafty statesman Charles Gravier, Comte de Vergennes, Foreign Minister for Louis XVI, had begun to discuss the possibilities of an alliance with Benjamin

101

Franklin, now our envoy in Paris for that express purpose. Aid had been filtering across the Atlantic under cover of a phony trading company, Hortalez et Cie, established by Caron de Beaumarchais, playwright, man about town, and dabbler in Revolution. Much of the powder burned by the Americans at Freeman's Farm was of French origin. Now the mask of undercover trading was off and France was in the war. Washington was not deceived by the look of victory somewhere along the horizon. His unfailing sense of the hard job immediately at hand forbade much dreaming of the sunshine somewhere in the future. He must still carry on the war with the little he had, never quite enough.

First of all there was Philadelphia. Benedict Arnold, the hero of Saratoga, was made Military Governor of that city, taking his oath acknowledging the United States of America to be free, independent, and sovereign states. Since Saratoga Arnold had fretted and rusted in comparative idleness crippled by the wound that he had received on his big day and nursing his resentment of the injustice that had been done him. Washington had included his name in the list of officers to be raised to the rank of major general, but Gates pulled wires with Congress and his name was dropped, the Congress pleading that the quota of major generals from Connecticut was already full. His appointment to Philadelphia was better than nothing, but it was not the active service that his restless spirit craved. Only in battle did he find his complete fulfillment.

Next to action stood Arnold's love of property and prestige. He had known these in modest measure in New Haven before the Revolution. In Philadelphia he soon found opportunities for the picking up of profit in ways that were not always legitimate. In spite of the scanty clothing and short rations for the fighters and the constant wails of poverty from Congress, it was a time of harvest for daring speculators in supplies, currency, or whatever offered. Sometimes the enterprises had a dangerous look of trading with the enemy. There were large risks, but the possible profits were larger. A realistic picture of this aspect of the struggle for freedom is not a pretty one.

His post as Military Governor made him a figure of considerable social importance in the city and his manner of living did nothing to obscure that fact. He chose one of the larger houses, the one that had been occupied by General Howe, and set up a four-horse carriage with coachman and footman and a house full of servants and entertained lavishly. If he had sought to give the impression of war profiteer he could hardly have contrived better. Soon he found Miss Shippen, the young lady whose father had refused André's offer of a part in the famous *Mischianza*, and Miss Peggy became the second Mrs. Arnold. His social position in Philadelphia seemed to be secure, but not so much could be said for his financial prospects.

Throughout his career Arnold was involved in controversy over money matters. He had been a poor accountant in civil life, given to counting his chickens before they were hatched and he was even worse in the army. He had performed gallantly on the ill-starred expedition against Quebec in 1775, taking charge after Montgomery was killed in the attack on the citadel, in spite of his own severe wound on that unhappy day. But Congress refused to be satisfied with his reports of receipts and expenditures through the winter and spring that followed. Again at Saratoga he had covered himself with glory in the headlong charge that broke the British line, but again his accounts were displeasing to his numerous critics in Congress.

As Governor of Philadelphia he had need to be especially careful to keep his public dealings clear of any confusion with his private affairs. He seems to have been quite the reverse.

A case in that point was his part in the purchase of the cargo
of a British ship brought in to Egg Harbor on the New Jersey
coast by a privateer. Here he fell under suspicion of using government wagons to haul the goods to the market in Philadelphia. Over a long period he wrangled with his critics. Again
his records were confused and obscure and remained so.

For Arnold it was always impossible to imagine himself
otherwise than as the injured party. The side he was on was
always the side of right and justice. His foes in Congress had
plotted to deprive him of the promotion to the rank of major
general he had earned at Saratoga. In all his correspondence,
even on quite different matters, there is a constant thread of
complaint of failure to appreciate his sacrifices of fortune,
health, and property in the patriot cause, scarcely a strong
recommendation to Washington whose own risks and sacrifices
were much greater.

In contrast with his tangled finances his courtship of Mar-
garet Shippen was swift, ardent, and effective and on April 8,
1778, they were married. The bride was not yet eighteen, the
groom double that age, with three sons from his first marriage.
A few days before the wedding Arnold, in spite of his protesta-
tions of poverty, had found the means for the purchase of a
large estate on the Schuylkill, Mount Pleasant, which he settled
on his wife for her lifetime.

Until quite recently there has been much controversy
among historians, professional and otherwise, over the genesis
of Arnold's subsequent course. Was he tempted by the British
with offers of large pay and high rank? Was he driven to the
point of betrayal by the bickering and ingratitude of Congress?
Had he always doubted the advisability of separation from
Britain? Was he really shocked by the alliance with France?
Who made the first overtures? The answers to these and other
questions were given only a few years ago in Mr. Carl van

Doren's authoritative *Secret History of the American Revolution*... In this book the story is told as it appears in the many letters and documents relating to the affair in the William L. Clements Library at Ann Arbor, Michigan.

On May 10, only a month after Arnold's marriage to Peggy Shippen, Joseph Stansbury, a merchant in Philadelphia known to be at least well disposed toward the British, talked with John André, the author and director of the *Mischianza*, the closing act of the British occupation of Philadelphia. André promptly and properly passed on the substance of his conversation with Stansbury to his chief, Sir Henry Clinton. In his talk with André, Stansbury represented himself as in Arnold's confidence and as speaking with the general's authority. In his memorandum to Sir Henry, André referred to Arnold as "Monk," suggesting that the American was prepared to play the part of the Scots officer who had taken his powerful Puritan army over to the Stuarts in 1660 setting Charles II on the throne of England. Prior to this time there is no evidence that any attempt had been made by Clinton or any of his agents to get in touch with Arnold directly or otherwise.

Other names used for Arnold were "Gustavus," "A. G." (General Arnold), and "Mr. Moore." A very simple form of cipher was used in the communications: each word was represented by three digits based on an agreed volume, such as Blackstone's *Commentaries,* the first digit indicating the page in the book, the second the line on the page, the third the number of the word in the line. Invisible ink that became legible under heat was used in most of them. All in all there was a melodramatic aspect to this traffic in subversion and treason that may well have appealed to André's sense of the theater.

There was a long series of secret negotiations, offers and counter offers, bargaining and bickering over terms, conditions, and prices that was to continue for sixteen months to its tragic climax in André's arrest, trial, and execution at Tappan, a village near Tarrytown, New York, in September 1780. The whole shabby story, with the activities of other figures large and small, is told by Mr. van Doren, writing with the documents before him. In spite of the hopes aroused by the French alliance it was a time of doubt and questioning. Many men played their small parts as spies for the British or the Americans, sometimes managing to stay in good odor with both sides at the same time. In New York the double dealers found a profitable market for their information. In some cases spies for Washington worked among the British, in a few instances, under instructions direct from Washington, conveying to Clinton news of American plans that were the exact reverse of the Commander in Chief's intentions.

Gage and Howe had had such shoddy agents in Boston even before the fighting at Concord. Espionage is an alluring art to restless souls who find the dull routine of life unbearable. Benjamin Church of Boston, skilled physician, respected citizen, member of the Massachusetts Provincial Congress and of the Committee of Safety, was a prominent member of the shabby tribe. A few of them prospered, others died. Of Church it is known only that he was discovered, confined in a Connecticut jail, released,and disappeared on a voyage to the West Indies. Benjamin Thompson of New Hampshire, long regarded as a sincere and respectable Loyalist, and who became a distinguished scientist abroad with the title of Count Rumford, was involved in this traffic, trading information to Gage for protection and a safe passage to England. William Herron of Connecticut was one of the double dealers, playing both ends in favor of the middle, which was himself, selling bits of gossip to the British as important news. He was one of those who came through unsuspected and stayed on in Connecticut serving several terms in the State Assembly and dying without discovery. John Vardill was one of the honest spies who served Clinton. All he asked was an appointment as Regius Professor of theology in King's College after the inevitable British victory. His was a vain hope. King's College became Columbia and there was no chair of theology for Brother Vardill. John Berkenhout stayed on in Philadelphia as a secret agent for the British after the evacuation. He seems to have dealt largely in diatribe and invective in his reports to his employers in New York. Congress was a group of "insolent demagogues," the Continental Army a "contemptible band of vagrants, deserters, and thieves,"—mostly Irish. The executive council of Congress "seemed such a club of tradesmen as commonly assembles in an alehouse in the borough of Southwark." In sharp contrast with this arbiter of manners and social position was John Honeyman who endured the maledictions of his neighbors as a "Tory butcher" and continued to convey useful information to Washington, including the vulnerability of the Hessians at Trenton which brought the Americans across the Delaware on that bitter Christmas night of 1776.

The wildest story of all was that Washington's rage at Arnold was really due to his bitter envy of Arnold for being the first to take the step that he (Washington) was contemplating. A man who could believe that could believe anything.

There is no need to trace the dragging course of the bickering between Arnold and Clinton. On Arnold's side it soon became clear that here was a greedy, shifty trader seeking a market for his goods, the betrayal of the cause to which he professed such profound devotion. His main concern was price. The chaffering between Arnold the willing traitor and Clinton the interested buyer was worthy the admiration of a shrewd Yankee horse trader. Sir Henry was willing to pay liberally in money and rank, but he must have adequate assurance that the goods were worth the price paid for them. How much of what could Arnold deliver? Still hiding behind a string of false names, he began by demanding a cash price of twenty thousand pounds in gold, with bonuses for losses on his American property, including a large grant of land in New York State which had been promised him but was not yet transferred. Mention was made of provision for his wife as well as for the sons of his first marriage. For this he would bring over with him a substantial American force, including a command which he hoped to have but had not yet received. He was never a modest bargainer.

The peak of his audacity was reached when he included in his list of compensations to be paid by the British his estimate of the pay he would receive if he remained loyal to his oath of allegiance. That the British should pay him for presumed fighting against them as well as for them was apparently too much even for Arnold and the absurd claim was not pressed.

After long delay and many disappointments Arnold was finally appointed to the command of West Point early in August of 1780. Now he had the goods in hand about which there had been so much sparring with Clinton. Soon an agreement was reached on price: ten thousand pounds sterling and two guineas per man for the troops turned over to the British. There were sundry incidentals — army pay and rank in his new allegiance, compensation for his property in New Haven, annuity for life for Mrs. Arnold, commissions for the three sons of his first marriage aged nine to fourteen. In all the final dealings John André, now adjutant general for Clinton with the rank of major, represented the British, calling himself Anderson in his communications.

The climax came late in September when Arnold and Anderson (André) met for the last time near Haverstraw

Mountain on the Hudson below West Point. The meeting was brief as the important details of the impending act of betrayal had already been arranged. There was discussion of the means and route by which André was to return to the British lines. It was impossible to go back by water as HMS *Vulture*, which had brought him had been fired on by a shore battery and forced to drop down river. André set forth early in the morning on horseback not in uniform but bearing a pass given him by Arnold. The other papers he carried were hidden in his boot. Near Tarrytown he was stopped by three horsemen, John Paulding, Isaac van Wart, and David Williams looking for Loyalist marauders who had been active the day before. Not saitsfied with André's explanation of his presence and purpose, they took him to the American post at North Castle. The commander there sent the captive on to Arnold, as he thought, and dispatched the papers to Washington. On the advice of Major Tallmadge who was more experienced in the ways of spies André was overtaken and brought back to await official decision.

From that point the action was swift. Washington promptly ordered a general court with Nathanael Greene of Rhode Island, now second in command to Washington, as president. André's statement at his trial was frank and open. The claim that he was entitled to the protection of a pass issued by Arnold he rejected as impossible. He at least understood his dilemma if others did not. The fact that he was not in uniform and without insignia of rank was damning evidence. The Court, after hearing the evidence, gave the sentence of death on the charge of espionage. Washington approved the decision of the Court and the end was at hand. The gallant André asked only that he be granted the right of a soldier's death before a firing squad. This Washington reluctantly denied and André was hanged as a spy, October 2nd.

Word of André's capture was carried to Arnold who received it while sitting at breakfast. Excusing himself to his guests he went at once to his barge waiting on the river and was rowed to the *Vulture* to be taken to New York and safety. His final shabby act was his insistence that the boatmen who had rowed him to safety be taken on board as prisoners. The army that he had plotted to deliver to the enemy boiled down to four boatmen.

In the little time they had the British worked hard to induce Washington to regard André as a prisoner of war and to deal with him accordingly, but to no avail. There was wide sympathy for André among Americans as well as British and many of the former favored an unofficial proposal that André be exchanged for Arnold at whose hanging his former comrades in the Continental Army would have been happy to assist. This of course was out of the question for Clinton.

Once Arnold was safe on the *Vulture* he lost no time in beginning the labored defense of his attempted betrayal which he was to continue as long as he lived. As soon as Washington learned of his defection and flight he hurried Hamilton off to overtake the fugitive if possible before he found a haven. The pursuit was too late, but Hamilton brought back with him a letter that he had dashed off on the *Vulture*, a masterpiece of self-justifications and smug self-satisfaction:

> The heart which is conscious of its own rectitude cannot attempt to palliate a step which the world may censure as wrong. I have ever acted from a principle of love to my country, since the commencement of the present unhappy conflict between Great Britain and the colonies. The same principle of love to my country actuates my present conduct, however it may appear inconsistent to the world, who very seldom judges right of any man's actions.*

How much did Arnold finally receive as the price of treason? The fact that he came alone into the British lines cancelled out the original price of ten thousand pounds sterling

Secret History of the American Revolution, Van Doren.

plus proven losses of property. There were many tangled threads in the long negotiations that followed. Mr. van Doren estimates that his final reward was somewhere between fifteen and twenty thousand dollars a year. If this was poverty it wat at least genteel. When Franklin learned of the affair he wrote Lafayette: "Judas sold only one man, Arnold three million. Judas got for his one man thirty pieces of silver, Arnold not a halfpenny a head. A miserable bargainer." Arnold's rank in the British Army was that of brigadier general with command of a regiment.

One thing that Arnold coveted almost as much as money was social acceptance and prestige. That Sir Henry could not guarantee. The British officers who knew disgrace when they saw it would fight alongside Arnold, but they would not treat him as a social equal, nor did they. One officer wrote: "It is a common saying at New York that the ship must be near sinking when the rats were leaving." Another reported that Arnold was "to raise a regiment of as great scoundrels as himself, if he can find them." After his retirement from active service Arnold tried hard to find employment in civil life in England, even beseeching the great East India Company, whose head pointed out with courteous contempt that that company could not deal with a candidate whose honor had been called in question. The company official to whom he applied was George Johnstone, late a member of the Carlisle Commission.

Arnold's military career with the British in America was short and without glory. In December 1780, he was sent to Virginia with a mixed force of British troops, Loyalist militia, and about a hundred Hessians. Once again in the field with an apparently free hand he displayed his usual ruthless energy. Prize money was scanty and he failed to achieve popularity with his troops. Fellow officers censured him privately for his greed. In New York it was said of him, "the love of money, his ruling passion, has been very conspicuous in Virginia." Superseded after a winter in Virginia he returned to New York for more restless waiting. In early September he headed a raid for the burning of New London in his native state of Connecticut. After that affair his troops complained that their own losses had been greater than those of the rebels. His life in England, whither he went near the end of 1781, was marked only by his efforts to gain the recognition that he thought he deserved. Finally he retired to a small house in the country and reconciled himself to his obscurity, as far as was possible for him. He died in 1801. Long before his death his name had become a synonym for Traitor in his native land.

CHAPTER IX

The War Turns South

Close on the heels of Arnold's treason came another happening that was disturbing to the patriots and briefly heartening to the British, the mutiny of the men and non-commissioned officers of the Pennsylvania Line, the Pennsylvania regiments in the Continental Army. The troops had had no pay for more than a year and in spite of protests and petitions prospects were gloomy. Finally on New Year's night of 1781 twenty-four hundred of them marched to Trenton on their way to Philadelphia to tell their troubles to Congress. It was surely the most orderly mutiny on record. No violence was offered and the march through the night was that of disciplined men in search of simple justice. Word reached Clinton in New York and he promptly sent two emissaries to urge the desirability of entering the King's service where pay was regular and the rations good. The mutineers turned the agents over to their commander Anthony Wayne who was following close behind them. Wayne convened a court martial on the spot and the agents were hanged. Arnold now in Virginia dashed off a letter to Clinton expressing his pleasure in hearing of the "revolt of so great a part of Mr. Washington's army." Later in the month a smaller number of New Jersey troops tried to imitate the Pennsylvanians. Two mutinies in a row were one too many and the mutiny was promptly suppressed by troops and the ringleaders were hanged.

It is easy to criticize Congress for its failure to provide the pay for the soldiers, but there was no adequate supply of money for civil or military services, then or ever, although French advances and supplies would soon begin to help. What was almost worse was the congressional habit of meeting appeals with moral exhortations commending the virtues of "patience and self-denial, fortitude and perseverance," advice hardly likely to please penniless and hungry men.

Treason and mutiny had little effect on the slow progress of the war. Arnold had come into the British lines an empty-handed fugitive, and his random service with the British had little value. If anything it only hardened the patriot resolve to fight to the end. There was no slackening of the recruiting effort by the Continentals and no visible increase in Loyalist enlistment with the British. In New York Clinton still hoped that a way might be found to capture West Point and thus cut off New England from the other colonies. While Burgoyne was following his destiny to Saratoga the British Clinton had beaten an American Clinton, General James, and had taken Stony Point and Fort Montgomery, but these were small posts of little value as long as West Point stood fast. Stony Point was the scene later of a desperate assault by "Mad" Anthony Wayne, mostly with the bayonet. Wayne said of this exploit later that if General Washington ordered him to storm hell he'd do it gladly.

When Arnold made his futile attempt to deliver the West Point garrison five and a half years had passed since the day of the Concord fight and the only point held by the British north of Charleston was New York. At sea they could impose a tight blockade when and where they wished, but on land they seemed helpless. If that seapower could be broken — but that was still wishful thinking.

So far neither side had paid much attention to the Southern colonies except to appeal to them for men and supplies for the Continental forces. Late in 1778 a combined attack was made on Savannah by a fleet sent from New York to join a force marching up from Florida under General Prevost. The defense of Savannah was weak and the town was easily taken and Prevost set to work repairing the crumbling fortifications. At this juncture there was a sudden gesture by the French which no one seemed to expect. Admiral d'Estaing appeared as though out of the blue with a large fleet of line-of-battle ships and transports carrying nearly six thousand crack troops and the men and siege guns were landed at the mouth of the Savannah River. General Lincoln, now in command of the Americans, urged immediate attack but d'Estaing ignored him and set about building siege works as though for the reduction of a major European fortress, calling on Prevost to surrender in the name of His Most Christian Majesty, Louis XVI. Much precious time was wasted in these formalities and when the attack was made it failed ignominiously, the gallant and useful Pulaski was killed, and the meticulous admiral headed for Martinique.

In the spring of 1780 the more important port of Charleston fell to the British after a brief defense and General Benjamin Lincoln who had foolishly allowed himself to be penned in the town in spite of Washington's warning against just such a course was a prisoner. Savannah was of little importance, merely the gateway to a narrow splinter on the southernmost edge of the rebellion. Charleston was quite another matter. Here was the largest center south of Baltimore and who held it might well control the southern half of the conflict. So the

British commanders reasoned as they reported that the war was over in the South. In reality it was just beginning.

It was a natural mistake for a British officer to make. Wars are fought by armies in the field and no Continental forces existed south of Virginia. Virginia and Maryland regiments were learning their trade under Washington in the North. The British could afford to ignore the bushwhacking that went on in the Carolinas between patriot and Loyalist irregulars. They could clean up that affair in short order when they got around to it. Local as it was this guerrila fighting was bitter and cruel. There were old grudges to pay and old hates to satisfy. The two Carolinas were fairly evenly divided between pro and anti and both sides burned and hanged and laid waste with equal vigor. After the Scots had risen in 1745 in a last desperate attempt to put a Stuart back on the throne of the United Kingdoms, the English rulers had banished groups of Highlanders to the wilds of North Carolina after a hard oath of allegiance under which they sacrificed land and life if they ever dared to lift a hand against the victorious government in London. The romantic figure of Flora MacDonald was among the exiles. These people were paying the hard price of unsuccessful rebellion and they wanted no more of it. Their part in the war was ended by the patriot victory in the short and bitter fight at Moore's Creek Bridge in 1776.

In the midst of the turmoil no one had time to consider the meaning of a victorious campaign in the Western wilderness along the upper Mississippi and the Wabash. In 1778 George Rogers Clark, Virginia born and acting under the authority of Virginia, took a force of two hundred riflemen down the Ohio to the mouth of the Cumberland and marched them overland to the small post of Kaskaskia, originally established by the French fifty miles down river from St. Louis. Kaskaskia fell without the firing of a shot. Then in the wet, cold month of February 1779, Clark led his handful across Illinois, wading over flooded prairies and crossing little rivers running bank-full, knee-deep, waist-deep, sometimes shoulder-deep, holding rifles and powder horns in their upheld arms, to capture the key post of Vincennes on the Wabash. It was a hard trip that only tough men could have made, and Clark marched and waded in the van. There was a wild, adventurous quality in the Clark blood. William, the younger brother of George Rogers, was the Clark who crossed the continent with Meriwether Lewis in 1805-6 to the mouth of the Columbia to clear the way for the later taking of Oregon. The capture of Vincennes was a bold challenge to British power in the whole middle region and was to be remembered when the time came to write the treaty in Paris, a clear sign that this was American land.

This was a new America and a new breed of Americans of which few British knew anything and most Americans little more, born beyond the mountains, knowing nothing of the older colonies on tidewater or of lands overseas. They could march fast and fight and endure and they hated discipline. In Clark they found a leader of their own kind and they would go anywhere he led. They would be heard from many times in the future. For the present they cared little about the war of which they caught only faint echoes. That was a concern of the folks "back East." Their own business was with the Britishers in Illinois and Indiana and they had taken care of them in the way they understood and liked.

In the meantime a ferment was stirring in the Carolinas. Clinton and his successor Lord Cornwallis sat comfortably in Charleston waiting for the expected rush of Loyalists to enlist under their rightful King. A new act was opening in the disorderly drama of the war in the South, a chapter that

usually receives scant attention in the conventional histories of
the Revolution.   It deserves much more.

The men who marched with Clark were not the only lone
fighters. They had blood brothers through the mountains of
Carolina and Tennessee, scattered over the small plantations
and around the swamps on the Atlantic slope, and their leaders began to appear, men with such names as Marion, Sumter,
Sevier, Davie, Shelby, Campbell, Williams, McDowell. Most
of the mountain men were hardened in Indian fighting but
they took little part in the war of the low country.

Of the lot Francis Marion, the Swamp Fox as the British
called him, was by far the most notable and the most persistent.
He was by birth, inclination, and experience a lowland planter,
of Huguenot descent, but not one of the Charleston aristocrats.
He had fought the Cherokees on their last foray into the low
country and had played a part in the pre-Revolutionary
movement, captain of militia, member of the Provincial Congress of South Carolina and of the Committee of Safety. But
for the fortunate accident of a broken ankle he would probably
have been with the prisoners when the British closed in on
Charleston. As an unenthusiastic member of what turned out
to be a drinking party he had seized an opportunity to go out
by way of the window when he discovered the purpose of
the meeting. His ankle was broken and he was carried back
to his plantation on a horse litter to walk with a limp the rest
of his days.

Marion's style of fighting was vastly different from that
of the professional soldier. He was the guerrilla pure and simple, moving fast with small bands, sometimes twenty or less,
following little known trails through dark swamps to cut up
small isolated British posts, ambush convoys of supplies, trap
Loyalist raiding parties in a sudden swirl of men and horses at
dawn. More than once he attacked with only three or four

rounds of ammunition per man; there was seldom need or time for more. He had no use for cannon, they were for the slow moving British, who were also the chief sources of food, clothes, blankets, and the precious powder and salt. Their horses were the rough-coated, scrubby, undersized native stock called "tackies." Dragoons scorned them as unworthy of a soldier's consideration, but like the men who rode them they could travel long distances over hard trails on scanty forage that would have killed the heavy, blooded stock that the British rode. They carried muskets, a few pistols, sometimes a rifle or two, and home-made cutlasses cut and hammered out of the blades of saws from country mills.

Marion himself carried only a cutlass, often rusted fast in the scabbard from which he seldom drew it. In an attack he gave his few orders with shrill blasts of a whistle more easily heard and understood than the spoken word. Most of the time his men followed him blindly, knowing nothing of place or purpose until the moment of assault. For rations on the march they had only what they could carry in pocket or saddle bag, baked sweet potatoes and lean beef, if they could get it. Many times the only advance notice his men had of an approaching raid was the sight of camp cooks preparing meager bundles for the ride. His men drank rum when they could get it, but Marion's only drink was water, preferably with vinegar mixed in it. This, by the way, was the drink issued to the men of a Roman legion on the march. Marion read little and probably knew no Roman history, but he knew the sustaining power of vinegar on the long gruelling rides through the dark. That much his experience and his common sense taught him, as they taught him most of what he knew about campaigning.

Marion was both a mystery and a perplexing problem to the British. Again and again they were sure they had him cornered only to learn of another blow at a distant post. This wasn't war as they knew it, close-ranked files of men in uniform facing each other at close range, firing in unaimed volleys and then rushing in to finish off with the bayonet. Catching this man was like grasping a handful of early morning mist; when the hand was opened there was nothing there. They wore no uniform except a round, tight-fitting cap, in the case of Marion with a crescent-shaped badge pinned to it bearing the inscriution "Liberty or Death," the motto of the South Carolina militia. If they were hard pressed or the fighting died down the men melted away into the swamps, becoming only so many country yokels, indistinguishable from other small farmers.

Marion's nickname of the "Swamp Fox" was given him by Banastre Tarleton the British raider. The story runs that Tarleton, proud of his ability to ride fast and hit hard, had attempted to match Marion in following watery trails through deep swamps where no trails could be seen and came out with only wet feet and tired horses for his reward. Disgusted and weary Tarleton announced that he was turning his attention to Thomas Sumter, another irregular who might give him a fight. "We will soon find the Game Cock (Sumter)," he remarked. "But as for this damned Swamp Fox, the devil himself couldn't catch him." The Swamp Fox could hardly hope to win the war, but it was he and his kind who kept it going until an army could be found.

After Philadelphia had been evacuated Washington was able to detach some of his veterans to serve as the core of an army in the Carolinas that might ultimately try conclusions with the British now under the command of Lord Cornwallis. As the best man to organize and lead such a force the Commander in Chief named his able second in command Nathanael Greene. Congress stubbornly ignored Washington's choice and picked Horatio Gates, the hesitant hero of Saratoga. It

is rumored that when Gates set forth in search of glory in
the South General Charles Lee who had once served briefly
and to no purpose at Charleston warned him: "Beware your
Northern laurels do not turn to Southern willows." The outcome of Gates's short and disastrous career amply justified such
a warning. Gates brought with him two regiments of hardened Continentals from Maryland and Delaware to set an
example for the inevitable militia, a few of whom from Virginia had had battle experience. The Carolinians were mostly
raw and unenthusiastic.

Gates quickly threw together a plan for a quick decisive
thrust that he hoped might even draw Cornwallis himself into
the bag to join Burgoyne. The blow that was to break the
British hold on the Carolinas was to be struck at Camden near
the center of South Carolina. Otho Williams who knew the
country advised a route through settled fertile country largely
friendly to the patriot cause, but Gates was eager to prove his
mettle against Cornwallis and insisted on a shorter route
through a region that had been fought over by irregulars of
both sides and was a desolate and hungry land, roadless and
townless with only dim tracks and an occasional poverty-strick-
en crossroads hamlet. The officers in council supported Gates
in the final decision in spite of all warnings, and the army came
hungry and dispirited to the battle for Camden.

The fight was brief and disastrous. The two regiments of
Continentals did their part in businesslike fashion and when
they withdrew from the hopeless melee they had given the
militia time to get away and scatter over the countryside.
Gates, the would-be conqueror, rode fast for comparative safety
in North Carolina, according to report riding nearly two
hundred miles in three and a half days without change of
horses. If the story is even almost true the credit belongs to
the horse and not the rider.

That was enough, even for Congress, and Greene started south to reorganize and recruit the broken army. The two Continental regiments were bitter over their mishandling and thirsted for another chance with a better leader. They found him in Greene. Nathanael Greene had shown his quality as second in command with Washington. He was called the Quaker blacksmith, although iron forger is a more accurate term. His family was a substantial one with a long record of useful public service in the tiny colony of Rhode Island, and Nathanael had been a student in what is now Brown University. Although born in the Quaker faith, he was probably better read in the history and art of war than any other man in the Continental Army. His Quaker brethren, disturbed by his study of war, dropped him from the meeting, without in the least interfering with his curious pastime. His reading went much farther than the records of forgotten campaigns. It is recorded that when he rode south to take over the command he carried a couple of volumes of Latin verse for diversion in his evenings by the campfire en route. He was held in high esteem by Washington and his fellow officers, as was shown by his being chosen presiding officer in the trial of the unfortunate André at Tarrytown.

Greene's meeting with Gates when he took over what was left of the Army of the South was short and apparently formal. It was a cheerless day in early December of 1780. An eyewitness said of it only: "It was an elegant lesson of propriety exhibited on a most delicate occasion."

What was the material of the army that Gates turned over to Greene? The rolls showed a total of 2,307 men, little more than two full regiments by modern military standards. Out of this number 1,482 were reported as present and fit for duty, 949 of them Continentals, the men from Maryland

and Delaware who had borne the brunt of the fighting at Camden and were keen to fight again. A more realistic statement gave the number of men fit and willing as less than 800, mostly Continentals. The rest were militia largely from the Carolinas who had broken on their first glimpse of British steel at Camden. It was from the militia that Greene must draw the material for the reorganizing of the army and the time was desperately short.

State authorities here, as they had been so often in the North, were more of a hindrance than a help in mustering the militia for Greene's aid. One official pleaded that he was so busy with his duties as secretary of the provincial council that he had no time for military affairs. Another reported that the recruiting orders had not been properly drawn and signed. Some ignored the call entirely. On the more hopeful side among the Continentals trained by von Steuben were men competent to help whip the raw material into a semblance of military ability. Discipline had been lax under Gates and after the rout at Camden virtually non-existent. Officers came and went at will and other officers were slow to report the offenders. Mild mannered and casual as he seemed, Greene was a hard disciplinarian and after one persistent law-breaker had been court-martialed and hanged chronic absenteeism without leave disappeared and something like a trained army began to take form.

Another change was in the new commander's attitude toward Marion and the other irregulars. Gates had treated Marion with scant courtesy, hinting strongly that there was no place in his grand scheme for such riffraff. Traces of this professional prejudice lingered on after Gates had faded out. An American officer reported his impression of Marion on his first visit to Greene: "Col. Marion, a gentleman of South Carolina, has been with the army a few days, attended by a

very few followers, distinguished by small leather caps and
the wretchedness of their attire; their number did not exceed
20 men and boys, some white, some black, all mounted but
most of them miserably equipped; their appearance was in
fact so burlesque that it was with difficulty the diversion of the
regular soldiery could be restrained by the officers; and the
General himself was glad of detaching Col. Marion, at his
own instance, towards the interior of South Carolina, with
orders to watch the motions of the enemy and furnish intelligence."

The truth was quite different from what the young officer
thought he saw. Greene knew all about the worth of Ethan
Allen and his Green Mountain Boys and Dan Morgan's riflemen from Virginia and he understood at once the sort of service Marion and his men could render. He made this clear in
a short letter to the Swamp Fox after their meeting at Char-
lotte: "Spies are the eyes of any army," he said, "and without
them a general is always groping in the dark, and can neither
secure himself nor annoy the enemy. At present I am badly
off for intelligence." Intelligence was Marion's specialty.
Unless he knew more of the British than they knew of him he
could hardly move a mile in safety. For the rest he was to
continue much as he had been, moving fast along obscure trails,
keeping the British off balance, forcing them to hold troops
in garrison posts when they were needed in the field, giving
Greene precious time for his recruiting and training. Thanks
to the instant understanding between the Quaker blacksmith
from Little Rhody and the lowland planter of South Carolina
with his ragged riders an army was beginning to take shape.

As has been intimated Marion was not alone among the
hit and run fighters who kept the war alive. Thomas Sumter
was another able and active leader of partisans, but probably
less effective than Marion. He resented orders and preferred

the lone war with no responsibility to the head of the army. In consequence not much was heard of him then or later. Occasional help came from the mountain men who slipped out of the wilderness valleys to give the British a taste of Indian fighting.

Something like that happened at King's Mountain on the border between the two Carolinas. Major Patrick Ferguson, a brave and able soldier commanding a mixed force of British regulars and Loyalist militia, led the extreme left wing of Cornwallis's long line of advance and had taken a strong position on the flat top of a mountain, defying all the "devils in hell" to dislodge him and his eleven hundred men. Williams, a mountain man, took him at his word and when Williams's force came over the rim of his mountain top fortress in the early dawn of October 1, 1780, Ferguson might well have believed that his challenge had been answered by a band of howling devils. The battle lasted all day and when it ended the British unit no longer existed — 456 dead the rest wounded or prisoners. Both Ferguson and Williams were among the dead. The fighters from over the mountains faded back into their hidden valleys.

There is a tablet in Greensboro that calls this the turning point in the tide of success that "terminated the Revolution." A turning point perhaps, but far from the last battle.

Daniel Morgan of Virginia was another free lance fighter in the war of the South, but his part was still different from that of the men who have been named. He had been a wagoner with Braddock in the Seven Years War and when he learned of the choice of Washington as Commander in Chief of the new army at Cambridge he led his long-striding mountaineers out of the Valley of the Shenandoah all the way to the siege of Boston. Arnold's march on Quebec attracted him and he took his men on the long agony of the Kennebec. He was at Arnold's side when they pierced the British front line for a moment of triumph. Then he was a prisoner for eight months, refusing his captor's offer of a British commission at the price of an oath of allegiance.

There is an unconfirmed legend that in declining the British offer of a colonel's commission he delivered himself of a few brave and well chosen words: "I hope, sir, you will never again insult me in my present distressed and unfortunate situation by making me offers which plainly imply that you think me a scoundrel." The doubter way well wonder what the tough old mountaineer really said. He was exchanged in time to take part in the action at Saratoga where Riedesel and his men heard the weird turkey call in the fringe of woods around the deserted fields of Freeman's Farm. After the surrender he went back to his farm in the Valley until the war in the South called him into action again.

The men who stuck with Morgan were hard, tough fighters, most of them young. The old battler had three prime requisites for his recruits: the ability to shoot, to march, and to starve. They soon learned that they would do all three. There were no baggage wagons, no reserve supplies, no tents. Each man had a gun, a knife, ammunition, a blanket, and a pouch at his belt to carry cornmeal; sometimes venison or sweet potatoes were added to the ration. Instead of using words of command he signaled to his men by blasts from a "turkey call," made from a bone of the wild turkey, a useful device with which all the mountain men were familiar. There was no pretext of a regular military organization and Morgan was the only officer. Usually they worked in small bands with leaders of their own kind who appeared when they were needed.

Morgan was an old man now and the hard years had taken heavy toll, but he had one more fight in his system and it was his best. In January, 1781, he met Tarleton, the ruthless raider, at a place called Cowpens near the South Carolina border. Cowpens owed its name to the fact that a cattle buyer named Hannah had built pens there for his cattle as he gathered them in around the countryside. Tarleton outnumbered Morgan heavily and had strong cavalry support and two pieces of light artillery.

Morgan deliberately chose the field for the battle, an open space surrounded by woods with a river in flood at their backs. Asked afterwards what he would have done if he had been forced to retreat he answered in forthright mountain fashion: "Retreat was the very thing I wished to cut off all hope of. I would have thanked Tarleton if he had surrounded me with his cavalry." The night before the fight he went among his men to show them how to sharpen their swords and joked with them about their sweethearts. Major Young who was there wrote of him: "Long after I laid down he was going about among the soldiers encouraging them and telling them that the 'Old Wagoner' would crack his whip over Ben (Banastre) in the morning as sure as he lived. 'Just hold up your heads, boys,' he would say. 'Three fires and you are free, and then when you return to your homes, how the old folks will bless you and the girls will kiss you for your gallant conduct.' "

Next morning the old man's boys responded gallantly and the arrogant Tarleton was lucky to get away, leaving behind him eighty dead, a hundred and fifty wounded, and six hundred prisoners. The American losses were twelve killed, six wounded, no prisoners. The mountain men reaped a rich harvest of loot, including the British band music. That was the end of the war for Morgan. Crippled by rheumatism he retired to his farm in the Valley to end his days there. Even the Continental Congress was moved to recognition of his contribution, a resolution of thanks and a gold medal. If that seemed slight to him he could console himself with thought of

Burgoyne's words to him after the surrender at Saratoga: "Sir, you command the finest regiment in the world."

Unfortunately Tarleton lived to raid again, especially in Virginia, where there are still echoes of his ruthless cruelty. His pride was in his ability to ride fast and hit hard without mercy. It is told of him that once catching a group of Virginia infantry in retreat he killed 113 of the militia, many of them lying on the ground helpless, and wounded 150. This exploit gave rise to the damning term "Tarleton's Quarter." His carnival of killing lighted a flame of resentment, even among former Loyalists, many of them peaceable Scotch-Irish farmers from Ulster. Not far from Charlottesville in Virginia there is a tablet with this inscription:

> Tradition says that under this oak the British cavalryman Banastre Tarleton pitched his tent on his road to Charlottesville, June 4, 1781. He attempted to capture Gov. Jefferson and the legislature, but Capt. Jack Jouett, by taking a shorter route, arrived in time to warn the patriots of their danger.

There is another tradition in that region which the present owner of a beautiful old plantation house likes to recall. When Tarleton was camped nearby, perhaps under that famous oak, the mistress of the manor invited him to breakfast. Tarleton came willingly to find the breakfast preceded by famous Virginia mint juleps. In consequence the raider missed his intended victim at Monticello. This too might well have happened, Tarleton's love of good food and drink being almost equal to his fondness for killing.

Some of the young Continental officers who had smiled at Marion and his ragged riders found themselves learning from him. Henry Lee of Virginia, "Light Horse Harry," destined to be the father of another Virginia soldier Robert E. Lee, a proud, ambitious, fiery plantation owner and graduate of Princeton College where he had Aaron Burr for roommate, was soon leading his horsemen, Lee's Legion, in wide sweeps around British held territory and bringing back valuable information, serving Greene as his distinguished son was later to be served by "Beauty" Stuart. The number and keenness of Greene's eyes was increasing.

While Greene was piecing together the wreck of the army that Gates had left, the British based on Charleston were waiting for the expected rush of Loyalists to enlist. It was unaccountably slow, although Clinton had offered what seemed to him generous terms; come in and take the oath of allegiance and all will be well, but still they didn't come. He tried again, this time with a proclamation advising the doubters that men of military age and fitness would be expected to serve with the colors. When Lord Cornwallis succeeded Sir Henry Clinton in the command at Charleston he too made proclamation, a warning that men who had served with the British and later skipped away to the patriot side would be hanged out of hand whenever caught. This impressive document made special reference to a "Mr. Marion" as a highly undesirable citizen.

Whatever the reasons it was clear even to the British officers that the countryside was not rising in behalf of their rightful King as had been hoped, the same puzzle that bewildered Germain in London. Evidently the King's forces must carry the war to the people if the people would not come to the war. No one could accuse Lord Cornwallis of being a laggard in war. The British had established a semicircle of strongly held posts stretching from Camden to Ninety-six, not far from Augusta, Georgia. Behind this line was another about fifty miles from Charleston to serve as a reserve in the unlikely event of need. The time was now late in 1780 and Greene was somewhere in the direction of Virginia, the goal that Cornwallis coveted.

This was to be a forced march for the British with as little baggage as possible. Speed was of the essence, and if they could come to grips with Greene the job would soon be done. It would be wearisome and confusing to recount the skirmishes and the minor fights, the marches and counter marches, racing for the next river in a region crisscrossed with rivers. Cornwallis did his best to set the pace but Lee's Legion and the horsemen of William Washington, a distant cousin of the Commander in Chief, hung on his flanks and threatened his rear guard, stinging him with swift stabs that never developed into battles but delayed him and wore down his men. Greene won all the races for the next river and took the available boats with him, giving Cornwallis another cause for delay. If he could only once bring the Americans to battle!

One fight there was that really counted; that was Guilford Court House, now Greensboro, North Carolina. In 1780 this was only a crossroads with a shabby frame building that served as the official center for the affairs of the county and two or three weather-beaten houses. This was selected by Greene as a good place to give the British a taste of the fight that they demanded. He took his battle position carefully with his army drawn up in three lines: first, North Carolina militia being given a chance to erase the memory of their rout at Camden; second, Virginia militia with many veteran fighters in their ranks, men who could and would fight; third, the hard core of Continentals who could not even spell the word "surrender."

The British attacked in a single long line with fixed bayonets. At sight of the oncoming close-locked ranks gleaming with steel the North Carolina militia broke again as they had at Camden and took to their heels without pausing to fire even a single round. The British line drove forward against the Virginians who took toll as the scarlet uniforms came on. The Continentals stopped the attack cold and as it turned aside the veterans followed Greene's orders and withdrew in good order. It was no part of the American plan to carry Cornwallis in

chains through the streets of Philadelphia or any other town.
Greene's business was in the Carolinas. If Cornwallis wanted
to follow the will-of-the-wisp Glory into Virginia he was quite
welcome. Greene was heading south.

Cornwallis issued a vainglorious report claiming a sweeping
victory with the rebels fleeing in all directions. Greene said
only that he would be glad to sell another field at the same
price. As Cornwallis headed for Virginia minus reserves and
baggage Greene took up the march south to clear the Carolinas. He had given Cornwallis his day of battle and his army
was intact and confident.

In spite of the unfortunate outcome of his fighting in
America, Cornwallis was probably the best of the British generals in this country. He thirsted for action and no one could
charge him with sitting quietly in a safe place and waiting for
the enemy to come to him, as did Clinton and usually Howe.
In fact he was sometimes too anxious to hear the clash of arms.
In battle he was gallantly impetuous and his men followed him
with utter confidence. He was to prove his mettle in India
later where his victories set his name high on the list of successful British generals.

Chapter X

Clearing the Carolinas

With Cornwallis out of the way seeking immortal fame in Virginia, and failing to find it, Greene was free to continue south determined to drive the British out of South Carolina and so out of the war. To the President of the Continental Congress he wrote: "I will recover South Carolina or perish in the attempt." It was not an easy task he had set for himself. Lord Rawdon had succeeded Cornwallis in command of the British forces in the Carolinas and still held the semi-circle of fortified posts from Camden to Ninety-six. To be sure Cornwallis had taken with him men who could have been used to hold the line or seek out the patriots in the field. The threat of a French fleet now operating in the West Indies had made the sending out of more troops and supplies from home uncertain, and there was no longer the illusion of recruits from Loyalists. Men who had hesitated and doubted were drifting over to Greene or to one of the irregular leaders.

Both British and Americans had unfortunate experiences with the colonial militia, whether patriot or Loyalist. The men who fought like wildcats when the war was in their own front yards balked at the idea of fighting under strange leaders in strange country. In sum total, however, the balance was in the militia's favor. Lord Cornwallis wrote to Sir Henry Clin-

132

ton, June 30, 1781: "I will not say much in praise of the militia of the Southern colonies, but the list of British officers killed and wounded by them since last June proves but too fatally that they were not contemptible."

Viewed in retrospect Cornwallis's thrust north into Virginia marked a change in the British plan of campaign. The capture of Savannah in 1778 had brought them little military profit. It gave them a good harbor but it was like a door opening into an empty room. The capture of Charleston was much more promising. Here was the center of the wealth and power of the Deep South. Who held this city held the Carolinas and hence the South. That had been the belief of both Sir Henry Clinton and Lord Cornwallis when they reported to the officials in London that the war in the South was over. Then Clinton turned the command over to Cornwallis and sailed for New York. Cornwallis in his turn gave the reins to Lord Rawdon, a commonplace and unimaginative officer, and headed north into Virginia to join with the traitorous Arnold in pacifying that sullen and restless colony. With control of Virginia would come control of the Chesapeake and that would really end the war. At the head of Chesapeake Bay was Baltimore and not far behind were Philadelphia and the Delaware. With these in British hands the "Old Fox" Washington would be in a pocket where he would have no choice but to surrender. It was beautifully simple, but would it work?

By the critical spring of 1781 the situation of the patriots seemed desperate. Cornwallis was wandering at his ease in Virginia with his base in the well fortified town of Yorktown guarded by British ships. Tarleton had transferred his attention to the Old Dominion and was giving the people reason to remember him. Although the French alliance was three years old the fighters for independence had as yet seen little cause for rejoicing over the addition of this ally. The taste of

French "cooperation" that d'Estaing had given at Savannah was a bitter one as General Lincoln had reason to know. To be sure money and credit had been made available and a few devoted friends had found their way to America, notably Lafayette who had become one of Washington's most dependable aides. There were other foreigners who had offered their swords to the cause, the gallant Polish engineer Pulaski who had planned the defenses at West Point and died at Savannah, de Kalb the man of mystery who had fallen with eleven wounds in the fighting around Camden, and von Steuben, late a drillmaster for Frederick the Great, who had made good use of the hungry winter at Valley Forge to teach the Continentals something of the art and practice of war. But these were individuals and it was armies that were needed.

The Americans had no navy although John Paul Jones had rocketed into unforgettable fame by beating two British ships, *Serapis* and *Countess of Scarborough* off Flamborough Head in September, 1778. The battle was so desperately close that when the British struck their colors Jones's own ship the *Bon Homme Richard* was sinking under him. He transferred his crew to the *Serapis* and sailed her into a French port. For all the rejoicing that word of his exploit produced in this country British ships still blockaded the American coastline from Maine to Savannah and British troops held Newport in Rhode Island. After much urging the French sent a fleet under d'Estaing to pry open the blockade. As he proved at Savannah d'Estaing was a master of hesitation and delay. A little effort would have put him off the mouth of the Delaware in ample time to block the British ships that were assisting in the evacuation of Philadelphia but the French admiral dallied and that chance was lost. He hesitated again off the port of New York and again he found reason for hesitation although he outgunned the British fleet by three to one. His masterpiece was achieved in the combined operation for the capture of Newport where French troops from the fleet were to join with John Sullivan who had a strong force of militia ready and waiting to attack on the landward side. There was a brief flurry of fighting between French and English ships off the entrance to the harbor interrupted by a northeasterly gale and the French headed for the large and safe harbor of Boston without bothering to put French troops ashore to join with Sullivan for the taking of Newport. The only fighting the French sailors did on this futile expedition was with American sailors in the streets of Boston. The time was coming when French ships would show their mettle against the British, but it would be under a different leader.

The problem of supplies was a chronic one and even when aid began to come from France the Continental Congress displayed its old ineptitude in organizing a working commissary. In Greene's army, as in Washington's, men marched barefoot over cold and stony ground. The chief sources of supply in the South were British convoys and isolated posts when they could be taken. When Camden was evacuated by Rawdon because of the need of men in active field service, Francis Marion found himself the possessor of a new suit of clothes, a rare article for the Swamp Fox. When Greene appointed Davie of Maryland as chief of commissary the latter protested that he was a fighter and knew nothing of money or accounts. The commander reassured him that there was no money and hence there would be no accounts. Apparently the business of the commissary was to collect whatever supplies he could and see to it that they reached the men whose need was the most pressing. There was no choice but to live off the country as did Marion and his men.

Part of the difficulty was the lack of specie, "hard money" the colonists called it. This was a long-standing grievance in

colonial history from the beginning. The British trading system, mercantilism, was directed toward the draining of gold
and silver from the colonial dependencies to pay for British-
made goods. This had been corrected in small part by the use
of Spanish and Portuguese coins picked up in trade with the
West Indies, mostly illicit, but these varied so greatly in value
from colony to colony that they were of doubtful service. Congress had authorized the issuance of paper money known as
Continentals, but the prospect of redemption in hard money
grew so dim with the decline of patriot fortunes that the phrase
"Not worth a Continental" became a term of common use.
At the lowest ebb of currency fluctuations such prices as the
following in Continental currency were common: a hat,
$400.00; leather breeches, $300.00; pair of shoes, $125.00; suit
of clothes, $1,600.00. When the troops were paid at all it was
in such worthless paper as this.

Through good times and bad Greene held firm to his purpose in the Carolinas, the ultimate breaking of the British grip
on Charleston. Before that could be accomplished the crescent-shaped line of posts from Camden to Ninety-six must be
pierced and the enemy driven back on the city. Now with
Yankee acumen he adapted his method to his problem and his
means. Marion had proved the effectiveness of the small, fast
moving, hard hitting plan of action. Keep the enemy off balance and in ignorance of place and time for the next blow. So
feinting and boring in and swinging off Greene avoided risking
the loss of his whole army in a single action, which had been
Gates's sin in his one battle in the South. Accordingly he in-
doctrinated his subordinate officers with Marion's concept of
hit and run. Even the spectacular Light Horse Harry Lee soon
caught the contagion and he and his men of the Legion became
willing pupils of the Swamp Fox following dim trails through

dark swamps, attacking at dawn, sending dim-eyed British sentries reeling in flight, gathering up swift loot, and merging into the landscape. In the twelve months from April 1780, to April 1781, Greene traveled over twenty-six hundred miles and fought a score or more of skirmishes large and small, two of which might well be called battles. Of this time Greene wrote laconically: "We fight, get beaten, rise and fight again!"

Names and locations of many of these encounters have long since been lost, but a few were marked by unusual circumstances. Fort Galphin in Georgia was taken by a clever ruse. For an obscure post it was strongly held, being on the edge of Cherokee country, and a head-on attack was out of the question. By a feint at an obvious point of attack the attention of the garrison was drawn to the threatened spot while the Americans drove in at the rear of the stockade. That was one of Lee's exploits, proof that he had learned his lesson well. The loot at Galphin included an unexpected windfall, nothing less than King George's annual "present" to the Indians awaiting delivery, ammunition, guns, blankets, rum of course, British gold, and most precious of all a supply of salt.

Marion's taking of Fort Watson, a small, strongly held post was another case marked for remembering. Here again a frontal attack was too risky and Marion set his men to building a tall tower of green trees cut from the surrounding forest, with a flat top commanding a view of the interior of the fort. Knowing the superior range and accuracy of the American rifle the British wisely capitulated.

The long rifles of the Americans were a mystery and a nuisance to the British. There may have been a few at Concord and again at Bunker Hill, but the fighting there had been at close range well within the reach of a musket. Now in the South the range and accuracy of the rifled gun began to count. At first this was just another of those smart Yankee tricks, not "really sporting, you know." Real soldiers stood up to each other at proper distance, often less than fifty yards, and exchanged volleys as gentlemen should. The *beau ideal* of this traditional method was the French officer who called out to his opponents: "You fire first, *messieurs!*" Naturally men schooled in this tradition were bewildered by an enemy who could pick officers off their horses at two hundred yards and even more. A few of the more observant reported to the ordnance authorities at home that here was a matter for thought.

The long barrel with the spiral groove in the bore was in reality a German contribution to the American Revolution. There were gunsmiths among the German settlers in Pennsylvania and in the Mohawk Valley of central New York. These men had learned their trade in the old country where curious-minded sportsmen had discovered that such a gun with the spiral grooves in the bore gave the small bullets that were used a rapid spin that greatly increased range and accuracy. That was the whole of the mystery. A backwoodsman who could knock a squirrel out of the top of a tall pine tree or kill a running deer at a hundred yards with a single shot was not likely to miss a British officer at a similar distance. Ordnance experts are hard to convince and it was nearly a hundred years before this lesson of the wilderness hunter was really mastered by the military mind.

There were riflemen, the *jaegers* (hunters), among the Hessians, but the methodical Germans froze the use of the rifle into the slow orderly European manual of arms with its fixed order and timing contrasting with the frontiersman's practice in which each man loaded, aimed, and fired at will, usually at a particular target preferably the white cross belts of an officer. Morgan's men gave Tarleton a taste of this kind of shooting at Cowpens. In reality, however, the riflemen played a comparatively small part in the Revolution. They were few in number confined chiefly to small commands such as Ethan Allen's, John Stark's, and Dan Morgan's. The major battles of the war were fought in the conventional manner with conventional weapons. Even in the Carolinas the chief weapons of the irregulars were craft and speed rather than guns.

On one occasion M'Ilwraith, a British major, made a quaint proposal to Marion, a duel between the two leaders in full view of their respective forces, an echo of medieval chivalry. Marion was no swordsman and knew it so he responded promptly with a counter proposal, a team affair with twenty men on a side, all mounted and armed with sabers and guns. To his men he gave instructions to load with buckshot, ride in fast, and give the other fellows a volley at fifty yards. He knew his men and their marksmanship from the back of a running horse and knew there would be little need for a second volley. This war was for keeps and not for exhibition purposes; there was no team match.

Colonel William Washington, who had been among the amused bystanders when Marion had his first meeting with Greene, lived to learn his lesson from the little man with the limp and was among those who threw swift attacks at the British flanks on the day at Guilford Court House. He captured a small British post not far from Camden by sheer bluff. A log mounted on wheels, a "Quaker gun," looked enough like a piece of field artillery to frighten the British into surrendering at discretion. This was not the only piece of bluff. Colonel John White with three soldiers at his back built a ring of fires to suggest a strong force poised for attack and Captain French of the British meekly surrendered three small armed vessels lying in one of the many rivers. With the vessels went their crews totalling forty men and thirteen stands of arms, all taken by an army of four men.

The fight at Eutaw Springs was one that deserved the title of battle. Greene was in on it with his Continentals and some well trained militia. The day went well. The militia gave a good account of themselves, even with the bayonet, the supreme test of the seasoned veteran. At the point of victory the militia gave way to their hunger for loot and while they milled around in disorder the British rallied and came on again. In the end they were driven from the field and success remained with the Americans. British losses, which they could ill afford, were heavy.

There was a touch of comedy that day. When the British reformed, Lieutenant Manning, finding himself a conspicuous target, seized a British officer as a shield, whereupon the human bulwark exclaimed indignantly: "Sir, I am Harry Barry, Deputy Adjutant General of the British Army, secretary to the Commandant of Charleston, captain of the 52nd Regiment, etc., etc." Manning's reply closed the incident: "Enough! Enough! You are just the man I am looking for."

This widespread fighting in South Carolina was the kind that the professionals neither knew nor liked. How could they beat an enemy they hardly saw, coming at them out of the watery darkness of swamps and trees, striking one hard blow, and then fading back as swiftly and mysteriously as they had come? The numbers engaged on both sides were never large, but for the British they added up to a steady draining away of strength. Sometimes enemy commanders sought to conceal their losses by sinking the bodies of their dead in the swamps.

Here is a brief sample from one of Marion's characteristic reports to Greene: "On Sept. 4 marched with 53 to attack a body of 200 Tories, who intended to surprise us — surprised a party of 45, killed and wounded all but 15; — met and attacked the main body and put them to flight though they had 200 men. . . . Marched to Black Mingo, Sept. 24, where was a guard of 60 men of the militia — attacked them on the 28th., killed 3, wounded and took 13 prisoners. I had 1 capt., and 1 private killed, 1 capt., 1 lieut., and 6 privates wounded."

Lord Rawdon found he could no longer hold the ring of posts from Camden to Ninety-six at full strength and at the same time maintain an effective force in the field with which to match the elusive Greene. Supplies were shrinking and soldiers were looking longingly in the direction of Charleston. Camden went first, May 9, 1781, the men falling back near the shelter of the base. Ninety-six was the next to go in this steady crumbling of their defenses. This had been a favorite refuge for the Loyalists who still hoped against the rising odds. When the troops headed for Charleston these refugees went with them, crowding into the poorer quarters of the city soon dubbed "Rawdonville."

With the British line of defenses broken and partisan forces riding at large over the countryside the men under Rawdon sat down in Charleston to wait it out. The French fleet was at sea somewhere near at hand and relief by water was too hazardous except as a last desperate resort. Greene lacked the men and the materiel for a frontal attack on the strong forces holding the city. The tide was running out for the British and time was fighting at last on the American side. By this time it was clear that the final throw of the dice would be at Yorktown where Cornwallis waited vainly for the coming of the fleet that Clinton had promised from New York.

With the British shut up in Charleston the war in the Carolinas passed from action to a state of uneasy stalemate. Greene's army was still ragged and hungry and lacked the stimulus of battle. Charleston remained in British hands while peace negotiations dragged on in Paris and it was not until the Treaty of Paris was ready for signing that the transports came into the harbor to take the last of the invading troops back to England.

There is a story, not too well authenticated, that as the boats pulled off to the waiting ships some rash observer suggested a final volley from Marion's troops to speed the parting guests. It was then that Marion pronounced his valedictory, so the tale runs: "My brigade is composed of citizens enough of whose blood has been shed already. If ordered to attack the enemy I shall obey, but with my consent not another life shall be lost though the event should procure me the highest honors of the soldier. Knowing, as we do, that the enemy are on the eve of departure, so far from offering to molest, I would rather send a party to protect them."

Marion ended the war as a brigadier general, a title he never used. When the British sailed away from Charleston, he said his brief farewells to his comrades in arms and turned back to his plantation so long neglected. Presently he married Miss Videau, the owner of an adjoining plantation. He asked no honors or rewards for his war service. There was a job to do and he did it. One of the officers, the trusted Peter Horrey, wrote a life of him afterward in which he had the dubious help of the ubiquitous and fantastically unreliable Weems. W. Gilmore Sims, a competent and reliable writer, did a sound life of Marion about fifty years after his death. Marion wrote nothing. Born a planter, he died a planter in 1796, laconic to the end.

For Greene as for Marion the evacuation of Charleston was the ending of the Revolution. South Carolina gave proof of her gratitude by voting him ten thousand guineas, much of which he spent on his army in picking up the arrears of pay due the troops. The rest went to the repair of his affairs in

Rhode Island which had suffered from lax management while the owner was fighting the war. Georgia promptly voted him a plantation that he might not have cause to regret his service to the South, and this became his winter home. With his beloved Kitty, who had waited patiently at home, he divided his remaining years between North and South, winters in Georgia and summers in Rhode Island, perhaps the first of the annual migrants now so common along the Eastern seaboard. He was only forty-four when he died in 1786.

CHAPTER XI

Building up to Yorktown

While Greene and the Irregulars were making life miserable for Rawdon and the British shut in around Charleston the war was shifting in the North. The treaty of alliance with the French had been slow in showing tangible results. The enthusiasm over the capture of Burgoyne's army was soon dimmed by Arnold's attempted betrayal and French supplies were slow in filtering down to the ragged, hungry men in the field. They were still cold and hungry and battle weary. Probably Washington's sad comment on the first news of Arnold's defection, "Whom can we trust now?" spoke the thought that was in many minds.

Overseas the feeling was more cheerful than in America. The enemies of England, which meant most of the continent of Europe, began to believe that at long last the pestiferous island across the English Channel was being brought to bay. Spain joined with France after much discreet prodding by Vergennes, the crafty French foreign minister. Spanish contributions to the cause were slight, but the mouth of the Mississippi River which Spain held was a good safe harbor for American privateers that were harrying British commerce in the West Indies.

While Franklin, with Silas Deane and Arthur Lee, was busy negotiating in Paris John Adams was in Holland urging the Dutch to seize this opportunity to extend their hold in the West Indies where they already had considerable interests. Next to the British the Dutch were the traders of the world and the little kingdom was enjoying growing prosperity. Finally in 1780 British pressure brought Dutch resentment to a fighting pitch and Holland was added to the list of powers that were openly on the side of the Americans.

Even distant Russia took a hand in the game of baiting the English with the League of Armed Neutrality proposed by the able and dissolute Empress Catherine. The principal effect of the creation of the League was to hamper the British efforts to control the foreign trade of neutral nations. If all these declarations of opposition to the British had resulted in outright military help the war might have ended speedily, but only the French really acted and even they were slow in making their hostility felt. The case of the French was special. The loss of their American territory in the Seven Years War twenty-five years earlier still rankled and they yearned for a slice of British trade, especially with the American colonies which British acts of trade had made closed territory to all nations except themselves.

Added to the military and commercial desires of the French was the enthusiasm of the intellectual circles of their aristocracy for the cause of liberty. That was the period in French history when large groups of thinking people were concerned to discover the true nature of Man; what he had been like in a state of nature before the artificialities of civilization had overwhelmed him. What was the Natural Law by which men lived? Condorcet and Voltaire hailed the American colonists as concrete demonstrations of their theories. To

Voltaire, hater of religious tyranny, Philadelphia had proved that men could live a good life in a state of religious liberty. Condorcet saw the Connecticut farmers living a simple life on the land free from the restraints of tyranny and proved his case in a tract with the amusing title of *Un Bourgeois de New-Haven*. Rousseau hailed the romantic reports of the life and ways of the American Indian as proof of the existence of the "noble savage" of his dreams. Here were natural men living as the laws of nature bade them. White settlers on the frontier would not have agreed.

To these men Benjamin Franklin was a welcome visitor from a simpler and wiser world free from the affectations and absurdities of a decadent society. Vergennes, the realistic statesman, the ablest in Europe, recognized in the old Philadelphian qualities of shrewdness and high intelligence while the charming society ladies among the *philosophes* sat at his feet and worshiped an image of their own making. To John Adams, his countryman, Franklin was a dissolute old roué. Franklin, knowing the transitory character of social favor, basked in the warm sun of his own popularity and worked steadily for more substantial forms of aid. The young and ardent among the men yearned to draw the sword for the new nation that was in the making overseas. To them the Virginia Bill of Rights and even more the Declaration of Independence were challenges to action. To be sure they were not indifferent to the possibility of high rank and good pay. Silas Deane spent many weary hours in Paris interviewing these willing workers and recommended far too many of them to the serious consideration of the Congress.

Washington listened to those who reached him and welcomed them in varying degree, but he seems never to have deceived himself as to the nature of his problem. For all the fighting and marching and enduring of his army the British would hold the upper hand as long as their control of the sea went unchallenged. How could the power of the British Navy be offset? By 1780 tentative and partial answers to this question began to appear. New Englanders were good shipbuilders and New England ports were filled with able seamen and captains itching for action. The Continental Congress was unavoidably slow in finding the money for ships and men, but a beginning could be made with privateers, armed merchant vessels that might outsail the heavy line-of-battle craft of the enemy and outfight the smaller.

From the standpoint of those engaged in it privateering was a business enterprise carried on for private profit. A successful voyage, which meant enemy merchantmen captured and sold in a neutral or home port, might well net a nice little nest egg for officers and men. Most of them promptly passed it on to tavern keepers and other more dubious establishments, but a few of the officers salted their gains away for later enjoyment. Most of the privateers hailed from New England, Boston and smaller ports and the thriving towns on Long Island Sound. About two thousand such craft were commissioned by the Continental Congress under the authority of a document called *Letters of Marque and Reprisal,* and at least three-quarters of them were from New England. Many of them were sunk, but others brought in cargoes of much needed sugar homeward bound from the West Indies destined for the British market. Privateer captains in general regarded fighting ship actions as an undesirable incident to the search for profit. As their number increased the British were forced to herd their merchant shipping into large convoys protected by the guns of line-of-battle ships and heavily armed frigates. Even so marine insurance in London on ships and cargoes from the West India islands rose to almost prohibitive rates. A few of the states experimented with state navies, but to little purpose.

The town of Marblehead in Massachusetts claims the credit for the first American man-of-war, the schooner *Hannah* commissioned by George Washington under the authority of the Continental Congress. Her captain was Nicholas Broughton and captain and crew were all men of Marblehead. The high point of the American Navy in the Revolution was reached in 1777 when there were thirty-four ships in commission and with the coming of the French the number dwindled rapidly to seven in 1782. Of the lot probably the most effective work was done by the *Congress* and the *Alliance* which were still afloat when the war ended. For all the smallness of our navy there are names that should be held in grateful remembrance, Esek Hopkins, Joshua Barney, John Barry, and of course the erratic genius John Paul Jones. Another daring captain was Gustavus Conyngham, whom the British called the "Dunkirk Pirate." He may have been the man who made his way into the Irish Sea and captured a packet boat making her regular run to Harwich and released her with a warning to the British that he was declaring a blockade of all the ports in those waters. Jones himself could hardly have surpassed that impudent exploit.

Jones's operations were largely confined to the English Channel with occasional forays into the North Sea or along the Irish coast, with his principal base at Brest. Once he attacked the shore batteries at Whitehaven not far from his Scottish birthplace. His major contribution was in the headaches he gave the British Admiralty with his harrying of coastwise traffic, but the news of his exploits that sifted back to America gave fresh heart to people who were hearing too often of American defeats. His fame has grown with the years and legend has been added to reality until it is hard to separate the true from the false.

The British sought their revenge by labelling him pirate and a poem by Rudyard Kipling, *The Rhyme of the Three Captains,* bears an explanatory note stating that "This incident appears to refer to one of the exploits of the notorious American pirate Paul Jones. It is founded on fact." Mrs. Molly Elliot Seawell in her excellent life of Jones writes that she has made a careful search of available records and has found nothing to substantiate such a charge. Mrs. Seawell was quite right. The poem has no historical relation to John Paul Jones, pirate or not, and Mr. Kipling is also right in saying that the incident is founded on fact. The incident referred to happened to the poet, not to the "pirate." Properly speaking the explanation has no place in a sober history of the American Revolution, but because the "Rhyme" has been associated with an American hero, however inaccurately, it is here told.

On his arrival in England with his amazing store of tales in prose and verse Kipling was much annoyed by the habit of certain American publishers of appropriating material published in England and reprinting it in America without payment or permission, a trick that was possible under then existing copyright law. Finally he freed his mind in *The Academy,* the leading magazine of literary criticism in England. This prompted a reply from the American offender — who must remain nameless in this footnote to history, although Kipling was not so merciful. The reply took the form of a joint letter signed by three well known English writers, Walter Besant, Thomas Hardy, and William Black, stating that they had had many and entirely agreeable dealings with this publisher and had always found him fair and scrupulous. But the poet had the last word. The "three captains" of the poem were the three authors named above who were the targets of the hot-tempered Kipling's wrath. Near the end of the poem is a cryptic line that is meaningless unless the reader has the clue.

We are paid in the coin of the white man's trade,
The *besant* is *hard, aye* and *black.*

The italics are by the writer of this note. And there, for the clearing of the record, is the secret of one Jones legend.

For all the efforts of the little Continental Navy, ably seconded by Jones overseas and the busy privateers cruising about the West Indies, the Brtish still held the seas in a tight grip and the blockade of American ports continued. Evidently more was needed and only the French could supply it. Washington at least was painfully aware of this. The treaty of alliance was signed in early February of 1778. It was typical of British stubbornness that eleven days later George III, yielding to the repeated urging of his Prime Minister Lord North, finally consented to a real offer of conciliation. At last the British were willing to talk terms: renunciation by Parliament of the right to tax the colonies, withdrawal of British troops except as they were requested by the colonies, repeal of all the acts of Parliament to which the colonies were objecting, including the Acts of Trade, asking only that the Americans should declare their allegiance to the King.

A year earlier this would in all probability have been hailed in America as a victory for the rebels. Even a month earlier it might have succeeded. When it came it was too little and too late, as was to be said of the action of another British administration more than a century and a half later. Now the French were in on the side of the American rebels and only complete separation or total defeat were possible.

The year was now 1780 and it was time for the French to show something more than money and supplies, important as these were. Above all French ships were needed if the cause were to prosper. Fortunately for the alliance the French Navy was in good condition, something that did not always happen. After their humiliating defeat in the Seven Years War they had reorganized their navy from top to bottom while the British Admiralty in the feeble, corrupt hands of Lord Sandwich was honeycombed with graft and incompetence. A huge line-of-battle ship, the *Royal George,* fresh from an overhauling and refitting in dockyard, capsized and sank in a quiet sea with the loss of all on board. Only the able Rodney represented the old breed of fighting admirals, and he was so burdened with debt and bedeviled by his creditors that he spent as much time as possible out of England. Meanwhile superannuated admirals, never noted for their competence, were recalled and put in command of battle fleets.

Not all the French commanders were of the top grade. Early in July 1778, Count d'Estaing appeared off the port of New York to threaten the British fleet lying in the inner harbor. The French ships were in good condition and officers and men were eager for a go at the enemy, but the admiral turned cautious and shied away from the prospect of running the gauntlet of the fortifications at the Narrows, that gateway between the outer and inner harbors, and gave orders to sail for Newport to take part in the joint land and sea attack with the unlucky John Sullivan commanding the Americans on the landward side. Later in the year he appeared unexpectedly at Savannah only to bungle the attack on the British there. That was the end of d'Estaing in American waters.

It was not until the summer of 1780, a year and a half after the signing of the treaty of alliance, that anything more was heard of effective military aid from the French. By that time the British had practically abandoned Newport as of

no military importance to them. The French had little difficulty in landing a well equipped and well trained force of
six thousand soldiers under General Rochambeau, an able and
eager leader, but Rhode Island was still far from anything
resembling war. Savannah and Charleston were now in British hands and the "pacification" of the Carolinas seemed to be
well under way. Washington was in the Highlands near West
Point watching Clinton in New York and waiting on the
events that were beginning to develop. French troops found
Newport a good place for vacation, making the acquaintance
of Rhode Island johnny cake and clambakes and dazzling the
eyes of farmers' daughters with their showy white uniforms
and ingratiating manners. It was pleasant but it wasn't war.

Months had passed in the attempt to build up an army in
the South that could dispute the British boast that the war there
was over. Gates came with his dream of a grand campaign that
would drive the enemy into the Atlantic only to see his dream
cut to shreds in the battle of Camden. Then came the methodical Greene to build an army that would really fight. Cornwallis met him at Guilford Court House and reported a sweeping victory over the American army that had dared to in-
terfere with his triumphant march into Virginia, the march
that was to bring these impudent rebels to their senses. Cornwallis, minus his baggage, moved on into Virginia to join with
Arnold who was there still in search of the glory — and the
wealth which he always seemed just to miss. In the Carolinas
Greene, who had brought his army out of the Guilford fight
with small loss, launched his long campaign that was to end when
the British took ship and sailed away from Charleston harbor.

In Virginia Cornwallis found a strong, well fortified post
waiting for him at Yorktown where the British fleet had a base
strategically placed for the control of the Chesapeake. The
American problem was still how to match the enemy at sea.

Washington stated it in a letter to Rochambeau waiting at Newport: "In any operation, and under all circumstances, a decisive naval superiority is to be considered as a fundamental principle, the basis upon which every hope of success must ultimately depend." In other words the key to victory lay in a powerful French fleet.

In the West Indies a strong fleet under the command of Admiral Count de Grasse was busy cleaning up. The orders to de Grasse were broad and flexible. When in his judgment affairs in the Caribbean were in order he was to head for that part of the American seaboard where he could render the greatest service. By that time the French were ready. In the summer of 1781 Cornwallis was in Yorktown busily strengthening the defenses there.

The plan developed rapidly from that point on. The year was 1781. In May of that year a small French fleet under the Count de Barras brought word to Rochambeau at Newport that de Grasse was sailing north that summer with a strong French fleet and the equivalent of three regiments of trained soldiers. Rochambeau had established good relations with Washington and promptly passed the word along to that commander waiting along the Hudson. The latter had assumed that the decisive blow would probably be struck at New York, but the final choice must be made by de Grasse who in turn must be governed by the necessities of supply. New York was more remote and offered the prospect of a long siege and difficult problems of approach and attack.

It was clear to both Washington and Rochambeau that if de Grasse chose the Chesapeake the combined French and American forces must march fast to keep their part of the bargain. The French admiral chose the Chesapeake and the army commanders started their troops on the long march south.

Now appeared another mystery of inaction in this war of
alternating battle and lethargy.   Clinton in New York held
a strong force in leash for the defense of New York, which he
believed was sure to be attacked.   Perhaps that was the reason
that he did nothing while the French were ferried across the
Hudson at King's Ferry only a short distance above New
York to join Washington's Continentals.   He continued to
do nothing while the two armies marched the length of New
Jersey wide open to flank attack from New York for days.   To
be sure by this time the combined armies were formidable in
size and in equipment, but it is a safe guess that Cornwallis
would have had a try at it.   It was on this march that Washington had three days at his Mount Vernon home, his first
glimpse of it since the first days at Cambridge.

It was August 30 when de Grasse anchored his fleet inside
Cape Charles and Cape Henry, the headlands that guard the
entrance to Chesapeake Bay.   The British fleet based in New
York had waited there too long under the impression that the
French were at Havana.   Rodney, the best the British had,
had returned to England taking with him four line-of-battle
ships, leaving Admiral Graves in command seconded by
Admiral Hood.   When the news came that the French were off
the Chesapeake they moved fast enough, and with favoring
winds were soon standing in for the battle that was to save
or wreck Cornwallis.   De Grasse stood out to meet him.   For
once the allies had the advantage in ships and fire power and
to make matters worse somebody bungled the signals and only
part of the British armada got into action at all.   That part
took a bad beating.

Naval historians seldom discuss this fight off the Chesapeake as among the great sea actions, but for the Americans
it was the decisive battle of the whole war.   With Graves and

Hood limping back to New York, Cornwallis was a prisoner in his own fortifications and time was running out. The end was in sight.

The siege of Yorktown opened on the last day of September. Rochambeau's heavy artillery had been brought from Newport on the small fleet commanded by de Barras who added his ships to those of de Grasse, making the waters of the Chesapeake secure against the unlikely possibility of another British attack from the sea. Now there was no lack of powder for allied guns and French powder was the best there was. It was more than three hard years since the treaty of alliance had been signed at Versailles, but now for the first time French troops and American Continentals were fighting side by side.

Cornwallis had what advantage there was in fighting behind strong, well planned fortifications, but the allies with about fifteen thousand, including Virginia militia now battle tried and reliable outnumbered him two to one. Only at Saratoga had the Americans had the upper hand in numbers. That was an ominous circumstance for Cornwallis. The climax of the siege was soon reached. Two redoubts of the defenders were carried in an assault by two columns, a French commanded by Lafayette and an American led by Colonel Alexander Hamilton. Throughout the war Hamilton had hungered for field command. Now he had it. He too was alien born. The illegitimate son of a Scotch planter on the island of St. Croix, he had landed in New York a friendless and almost penniless immigrant at the age of fifteen and at once enrolled as a student in King's College, soon to become Columbia. Dislike of British control was no new thing to young Hamilton. The planters of St. Croix as on other British islands had chafed under the burden of the British laws of trade. As the clouds of the Revolution gathered he took an

active part in the debate engendered by the action of the Stamp
Act Congress and when the Continental Army began to take
shape he promptly joined up hoping to have command of the
artillery. Fate had decreed otherwise but now at Yorktown
he was to have the honor of marching at the head of the
American column in the assault.

The redoubts were taken at the point of the bayonet and
after a futile attempt to slip away across the York River Cornwallis had no option but to surrender. General O'Hara delivered the British General's sword which was received by
General Lincoln as a consolation for his own surrender at
Charleston. There was a touch of comedy. As the British
soldiers marched through the allied lines their bands played a
popular melody of the time, *The World Turned Upside Down*.
For once the Continentals wore new uniforms paid for with
French gold. That night messengers rode hard toward the
north spreading the news and in the early morning wakeful
citizens in Baltimore and Philadelphia heard night watchmen
crying the hour along empty streets, adding the joyful news,
"And Cornwallis is taken!" Lafayette wrote to Vergennes in
Paris: "The play is over, Monsieur le Comte." A tablet marking the spot where the surrender took place bears this curt
inscription: "On this spot Lord Cornwallis commanding the
British forces surrendered to General Washington, Oct. 19,
1781." The fighting was over, but peace was still two years
away.

After the surrender the American commander was host
to Cornwallis and his officers at American headquarters. In
responding to a toast by Washington Cornwallis harked back
to the hard days on the Brandywine and at Valley Forge when
the continuance of the war hung on the will of the Virginian:
"When the illustrious part that your excellency has borne in

this long contest becomes matter of history, fame will gather your brightest laurels from the banks of the Delaware rather than from those of the Chesapeake." For the men who remembered Valley Forge, Yorktown had been a pleasant pastime.

CHAPTER XII

Victory but not yet Peace

Two years of comparative quiet followed the victory over Cornwallis. It was in reality a stalemate, neither peace nor war. The British Government, having lost two armies in America, had no stomach for further fighting, but they still held New York with large bargaining advantages in the long negotiations that were to come before the treaty of peace would be ready for signing. And there were other British interests in America that might be saved out of the wreck.

The British were not the only people who were concerned in the ultimate outcome of this strange war. Spain, a laggard in the fighting, was determined to keep control of the Mississippi from New Orleans at the mouth, and France, still our ally but now also our rival, had a large stake in the sugar islands of the West Indies and was entertaining dreams of a share in the Wild Lands between the Alleghenies and the Mississippi. Vergennes, the French Foreign Minister, came forward with a nice offer, nothing less than a division of that area between France and Spain, of course with treaties of amity and concord between themselves and the new United States. European powers are skillful in dividing land in countries about which they know little or nothing.

Then there were always the British, smarting from their loss of another army and desperately needing rest and time to recover. They still held fortified posts in the Western country, especially on the Great Lakes, seven in all, two on Lake Champlain, Dutchman's Point and Pointe-au-Fer, guarding the route to Montreal, Oswegatchie on the upper St. Lawrence, Oswego on Lake Ontario, Niagara on the American side of the river, Detroit in a strong position on the river connecting Lake Erie with the north, and the island of Michilimackinac at the upper end of Lake Michigan. The position of these posts reveals the nature of one important interest of the British; these were guard-posts of the trade between the Ohio country, as it was then called, and the British in Canada. The capture of Canada from the French with the surrender of Montcalm at Quebec in the Seven Years War had given the rich fur trade into British hands. An average of two hundred thousand pounds sterling worth of furs passed through Montreal each year, most of them bound for London. If they could hold control of the chief gateways through which this trade passed they might yet win the war, especially if this became the entering wedge for the retention of all the foreign trade with the late colonies. Naturally European countries interested in the trade, especially France and Holland, failed to see eye to eye with the British. All in all it was a nice little tangle with revenge, jealousy, and greed making their appropriate contributions.

The existing boundaries and status of the area between the Great Lakes and the Ohio River were highly uncertain. After the Seven Years War the victorious British, seeking to simplify the administration of the affairs of the French people around Quebec and Montreal had extended the boundaries of the Province of Quebec to the Ohio. A Proclamation prepared by the friendly hand of Lord Shelburne in 1761 had drawn a line along the crest of the Alleghenies in western Pennsylvania, forbidding settlers and traders with the Indians from crossing it. Shelburne hoped to allay American resentment by assuring the colonists that this was only a temporary measure which would be mitigated as soon as the British Government had had time to set up a system for licensing traders and settlers. Then Shelburne was forced out of office and his successors promptly forgot the promise. Settlers and traders continued to trickle through the paper barrier, to the great annoyance of the Shawnees who believed it to be their land that was at stake, and the tomahawk and torch came into play. The Shawnees were an able and warlike people who did not enjoy being pushed around, especially by the British or the Americans, whom they particularly disliked and distrusted. To complete the confusion and general ill will the fur trade originating in this middle country was not to be ignored.

If only the British played their cards skilfully at Whitehall the territory that now contains the states of Ohio, Illinois, Indiana, and Michigan might be held permanently as a valuable fur trading and hunting preserve. In spite of their experience at Saratoga and Yorktown the British were slow to understand the dynamic nature of American growth. The idea that American settlers hungry for new land would be willing to bypass such an opportunity as the Ohio country presented was an absurdity everywhere — except in a government office remote from the realities of land and people.

Before the surrender at Yorktown two imperial heads in Europe, the Emperor of Austria and the Empress of Russia, had pushed forward with offers of their good services as mediators. John Adams now in Paris was almost beside himself with rage at such effrontery and George III felt his own dignity to have been injured. That ended that rather absurd proposal and with the news of Yorktown Lord North, pliant agent of the royal will in London, finally succeeded in resigning when the King repeated his stubborn refusal to consider the loss of the American colonies. Lord Rockingham succeeded North and an English emissary was sent to Paris to sound out the shrewd Franklin. The latter craftily suggested the turning over of Canada to the victorious Americans. That of course called for further negotiation and delay and probably softened the British objection to bargaining. At the moment there were still nearly thirty thousand British troops scattered along the coast from Quebec to Savannah, doing nothing at all at large expense . . . Savannah and Charleston were not evacuated by the British until July and December respectively of 1782.

In spite of the general exultation over the surrender of the British at Yorktown the fighting power of the Americans was at low ebb, as Washington knew well. Without French troops and ships they were weaker after Yorktown than they were before and Clinton at New York was strong enough to crush the Continentals if he could shake off his lethargy and take the field. While the French fleet held the Chesapeake that part of the coastline was secure, but the real interest of our ally was in the West Indies. Admiral Rodney returned to meet and overcome de Grasse in Caribbean waters in the famous battle of the Saints in April of 1782. A combined sea and land attack by the Spanish and French on the fortifications at Gibraltar was beaten by the small garrison there and the British still held the seas.

As an incident to the war the British had taken Florida from the Spanish adding another knot to the tangle in American affairs. There as elsewhere boundaries were uncertain, particularly in West Florida, that strip of territory that stretches westward along the Gulf coast beyond Pensacola. How far did it stretch? The answer varied with the political ambitions and prejudices of the individual. When Spain held both Florida and Louisiana the matter of western limits was of no importance, but now control of the mouth of the Mississippi was of major concern. Trade down the great river was growing steadily and Americans were soon to demand at least free navigation and trade at New Orleans, if not outright ownership. Standing alone Spain could be brushed out of the way easily, but not in a peace conference if it ever came to that.

Natchez, now a picturesque old town in Southern Mississippi sleeping peacefully on the heights above the empty river, can point with pride to the fact that in those troubled days flags of four nations, England, Spain, France, and the United States had flown there. To these should be added the Stars and Bars of the Southern Confederacy which floated there through the four years of Rebellion. It is no longer a key point and its people are content with their old houses and their beautiful gardens.

The chief weakness of the British was in their own government. Opposition to the war had been unceasing in Parliament and with Lord North out of the way it became stronger. The strength of the Americans was that separation from England was now a fact beyond change. Only George III could still hope that the erring colonial lambs would yet return to the fold.

Negotiations dragged along in Paris where five commissioners were representing America instead of the capable Franklin alone. Two new men on the job were John Adams and John Jay. Jay was constitutionally suspicious of all foreigners, especially the French and English. Franklin had seemed willing to follow the lead of Vergennes who spoke for the French interest of course, and Jay was aware of the attempts of the French minister in Philadelphia to separate the trans-Appalachian region from the seaboard states and permit the French, Spanish, and even British to carve up the vast interior region to suit their conflicting plans. Jay had less reason for suspicion of Lord Shelburne, who had by this time succeeded Rockingham as Prime Minister. Perhaps he listened too much to the phrase that Fox applied to Shelburne, "the Jesuit of Berkeley Square." His charge that Vergennes was guilty of double dealing had foundation, but the latter might argue that his government had promised independence for the Americans, with no provision as to boundaries.

Some of the negotiators were almost as anxious to save "face" as to grab land. One of the British emissaries was authorized by Shelburne to treat with commissioners of the colonies "under the title of Thirteen United States." Perhaps it was thought that such a phrase might make the Americans seem less united and independent. Fortunately the Americans decided to regard this as a recognition of their complete independence so no harm was done.

In spite of all the agreeing and disagreeing, the promising and the double crossing, a preliminary treaty was signed November 30, 1782, to become effective when England and France had made peace. These two powers dawdled and argued and it was not until September 3, 1783, that the final treaty was signed in Paris and the war was over. Congress had officially proclaimed the cessation of hostilities between England and the United States some months earlier, on April 19, 1783, the anniversary of Lexington and Concord. Eight tumultuous and dangerous years lay between that brief scuffle at the bridge and this official proclamation of the end of the war.

After the evacuation of New York following the signing of the treaty, Washington met his officers at Fraunces
Tavern, still preserved as a shrine in New York's financial
district, spoke a few words of solemn farewell to these men,
many of whom had come all the way with him, and set out
on the long trip back to Mount Vernon where he hoped to
spend the rest of his days rebuilding his long neglected fields.
For all of them the war had been an interruption and an ordeal,
but there had been companionship for them and occasional
gleams of triumph. They had come out of civil life and were
now going back to it. Doubtless they felt that they knew
the best and the worst about each other. Presently an organization of these young officers would appear, the Order of
Cincinnati, but on that last day they can have had little
thought for anything but the stupendous fact that the war
was over and they were soldiers no longer. For their commander there was only praise and deep respect. Few men
have ever given such distinguished and unselfish service to
their fellows as had he, thirty years of it. Now he asked only
the quiet peace of his farms.

What were the terms of the Treaty of Paris as finally
agreed to and signed? Considering that the British still held
New York and seven key posts around the Great Lakes, they
were on the whole surprisingly favorable to the Americans.
The French fleet had withdrawn to the West Indies where
Rodney was soon to give them a crushing defeat. The French
troops had gone with the fleet and the fighting power of the
Continental Army was low. At first thought the British had
only to sit tight where they were and the colonial cause was
bound to wither. But the British were as war weary as were
the Americans. Furthermore it seemed to some of the people
at Whitehall that it would be comparatively simple to hold
the American trade even without political control. Thus they

would be free from the growing cost of colonial establishment and reap a rich harvest from the trade of the new nation. Like other British dreams this proved to be an illusion, but it played its part in increasing their willingness to recognize the new United States.

To the American commissioners the clause in the treaty stating the fact of recognition in unmistakable terms was the one that was of supreme importance. By contrast the other articles were of minor significance. Many of the terms as laid down in the final document were vague and subject to various interpretations, especially those relating to boundaries. The northeast boundary between what was then the Province of Maine and what is now New Brunswick remained vague until it was settled by Daniel Webster and Lord Ashburton sixty years later. In the South England returned Florida to Spain, salving Spanish disappointment over her failure to take Gibraltar. Otherwise boundary lines in that region remained as confused and uncertain as they had been. Those points were removed from the field of controversy by the American purchase of the Louisiana Territory from France in 1804 and of Florida from Spain in 1819. There was little dispute over the northern boundary along the Saint Lawrence and through the Great Lakes, but nothing was said about the posts still held by British troops in that area. Thanks to John Adams the Americans kept the fishing rights they had held as colonials in the waters around Nova Scotia and Newfoundland.

A matter which provoked much discussion was the settlement of private debts of which there were many. British merchants resurrected from their files bills for goods sold to the colonists before the war. And there were the confiscated estates of Loyalists in America. These were now the property of the various states that had been prompt to pick them up and sell

them to settlers. To illustrate, the Johnsons claimed a princely domain in the Mohawk Valley in New York roughly estimated at a million acres and the Penns still claimed the whole
state of Pennsylvania under the terms of the grant from Charles
II.

Here was a very thorny problem. The only central government in the new nation was the Continental Congress and
this body lacked money to pay the bills and had no power to
compel the states to do it. In the end Franklin proposed that
the Congress should "earnestly recommend" that the states
assume responsibility. This plan was without meaning or
force, as Franklin well knew, but it satisfied Parliament and
harmed no one except the former owners of the land. Only
Pennsylvania heeded the earnest recommendation and paid
the Penn family $650,000 for their lost American barony, not
a bad bargain for Pennsylvania since the land in question was
the whole state. Add to this list the fact that both parties
retained the right of free navigation of the Mississippi. There
in substance is the Treaty of Paris that ended the Revolutionary
War.

ILLUSTRATIONS

THE BOSTONIANS PAYING THE EXCISEMAN, OR TARRING AND FEATHERING.

PLATE I

Paying the Exciseman, c. 1773

PLATE II

A view of the town of Concord, 1775

PLATE III

Lee taken by Harcourt, Morris County, 1776

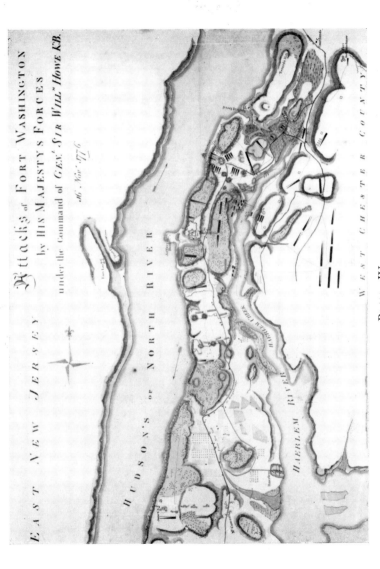

PLATE IV

Howe's forces at Fort Washington, 1776

PLATE V

Plan of the Battle of Yorktown, 1781

PLATE VI

Cornwallis surrenders to Washington and Count de Rochambeau,
Yorktown, 1781

CHAPTER XIII

The Confederacy Breaks Down

There was good reason behind the term "Thirteen United States" that British negotiators had used. As has been shown the separate states had been prompt to adopt constitutions and set up in business for themselves, some of them even before the Declaration of Independence was signed in Philadelphia. All of them assumed the airs of sovereignty and exercised many of the functions. The Continental Congress was a voluntary organization the members of which more nearly resembled ambassadors from the separate states than national legislators. The Articles of Confederation under which the Congress operated declared in the preamble that the purpose is a "perpetual union," but of what was it a union? The second article gives the answer by its declaration that "Each state retains its sovereignty, freedom, and independence." Article III calls this union "a firm league of friendship." The individual states retained control of taxation and commerce, important functions of any government. The Congress could request — "requisition" was the word used — contributions from the member states, but it could not collect the money or material needed nor could it punish the laggards. The states stood on equal footing in the Congress with one vote each, whatever the number of delegates from any of them. Amendment of these Articles of Confederation required a unanimous vote. Naturally there were no amendments. When one considers the immensity of the problems that the war brought and the limited power of the Congress to deal with them the wonder is not that they did so badly but that they did so well.

The Articles were agreed to by the Continental Congress, November 15, 1777, but were not ratified and put in force until March 1, 1781. The reason for this long delay was the refusal of Maryland to agree to any form of political union until the question of the ownership of the so-called Wild Lands between the Alleghenies and the Mississippi had been settled. Georgia, the Carolinas, Virginia, New York, and Connecticut claimed a share in the lands under their colonial charters. Often these claims overlapped and two or three states laid claim to the same area. New York and New Hampshire both claimed Vermont as a rightful part of their original grants and were at the point of war. Under the leadership of the outspoken and belligerent Ethan Allen Vermont solved that problem by declaring herself independent of both blusterers and set up a government of her own which patriotic Vermonters like to remember as the "free and independent Republic of Vermont." On the 16th of February, 1791, the newly created Congress of the United States admitted her to the Union as the fourteenth state.

There were boundary disputes between most adjoining colonies. Little Rhode Island was kept busy fighting off the encroachments of her neighbors Connecticut and Massachusetts, Virginia and North Carolina were in sharp dispute over the exact location of the dividing line between them. Early surveys had been uncertain and vague in their definitions of land limits and maps were too often offhand flights of the map-maker's imagination. An important case was the line between Virginia and Maryland. This was to have unexpected results which call for later examination.

Under the terms of the Articles of Confederation the Congress was "the last resort on appeal in all disputes and differences . . . between two or more states concerning boundary, jurisdiction, or any cause whatsoever," but Congress was slow to act, and procedures were uncertain, so no use was made of this provision by any of the contestants. They preferred to fight out their differences in their own way. As might have been expected there were few agreements.

No provision was made for a President or any other kind of a Chief Executive, nor were any courts set up to have any kind of overall jurisdiction. The only courts were those in the separate states. The president of the Congress was chosen by the delegates themselves and his functions were limited to presiding over the meetings of the members. While the war lasted these omissions and shortcomings in the Congress seemed to make little difference except in the operation of the commissary and the appointment and promotion of officers. Here there were many charges of favoritism and discrimination.

Shortcomings that had seemed unimportant during the heat of conflict became matters of major concern now that peace had been achieved. Boundary disputes were neither the only nor the most pressing of the questions that arose. There were the debts, public and private, domestic and foreign. Most urgent of all were the sums owed to France for money loaned. In 1783 the total foreign debt, mostly to the French, was approximately eight million dollars and since the Congress was unable to pay the interest as it came due the amount was increasing annually. After the emotional pressure of the war had ended the sums paid in by the states to the feeble central government averaged around half a million dollars a year, hardly enough to pay the regular expenses of such government as there was, with nothing over for the debt to France.

This was only the beginning; there were debts owed by the government to individuals for supplies furnished during the war. States had borrowed money in various ways, by the issuance of "bills of credit," little more than notes promising to pay at some future date, money borrowed on land owned or claimed by the borrower, money borrowed by the simple expedient of failing to pay bills when they fell due. It was all such a hopeless tangle of debts and claims and promises that the total sum involved is hard to find. On top of the growing heap of plain debts owed by the Continental Congress and the various states both Congress and the states had issued paper money to take the place of the gold and silver currency that practically did not exist. The total amount of paper currency issued by Congress in this manner was $245,000,000; the states put out $210,000,000, a grand total of nearly half a billion. If these dollars had been worth the amount printed on the bills the daily operations of finance and trade would have been simple enough, but as the money rolled off the presses the value went down. At the low point forty dollars in continental currency were required to equal one dollar in gold or silver, and some of the state issues were even lower, often refused at any price outside the state of issue.

About the time of the victory at Yorktown Robert Morris of Philadelphia, a successful and patriotic merchant, undertook the thankless task of acting as Superintendent of Finance for Congress. He was able to cut down waste and corruption, reformed the accounting and administrative methods, and improved the system of purchasing supplies so that the Army at long last was almost decently fed and clothed, but the finding of additional revenue was beyond the power of even Robert Morris. Gold and silver for a national treasury were simply not to be had. The only hard money was that from France plus specie spent by French and British troops fighting in America. After a year of fruitless effort Morris resigned in despair, lamenting that our public credit was gone. In his letter of resignation he said: "Talking to the states is like talking to the dead," declaring that he resigned rather than continue as "the minister of injustice."

The world of today is painfully familiar with taxation as an obvious method of raising money for the expenses of government of every kind, national, state, and local, but in the American world of 1780 that road was closed to the Continental Congress. The Articles of Confederation had given the power to request but not to demand. State governments, however, were not so limited. The power of taxation was theirs and some of them used it to the full, taking the land or other property of the delinquent if he failed to pay his tax bill.

Massachusetts was the scene of an incipient war that threatened the existence of the state government, known in history as "Shays' Rebellion." The state constitution gave the commercial people of the cities, chiefly Boston, the power to lay the tax burden most heavily on the people who were least able to bear it, particularly the farmers. In addition there was a heavy tax on the individual, called a poll tax, or head tax, in some cases amounting to forty per cent of the amount claimed by the state. Farmers were without money and the courts were soon filled with suits brought by the state for the taking of the farmers' lands. In some cases the state claimed arrears of taxes over a period of five years and pressed hard for payment.

Finally the farmers in the Berkshires in the western part of the state rose in revolt, feeling themselves goaded beyond endurance. Many of them had fought bravely at Bennington or Saratoga and remembered the deep resentment of the taxes imposed by the British. Was not this one of the reasons for the Revolution? They found a leader, albeit an unwilling one, in the person of Daniel Shays who had given a good account of himself in the fighting as a captain of Massachusetts militia.   At first they confined themselves to efforts to prevent the local courts from sitting for the trial of tax cases. The state promptly declared them outlaws, as they were legally, and ordered them to disperse.   The rebels, armed mostly with pitchforks and improvised pikes, having little ammunition for their old muskets, attacked the arsenal at Springfield where there were stores of ammunition as wall as arms.   This was war and the militia were called in to suppress the rebellion and there were loud calls for the hanging of the leaders, especially Daniel Shays. Cautions, ambitious John Hancock, the Governor, resigned rather than face the storm and his successor, stout-hearted James Bowdoin, was wiser than the counselors of revenge.   No one was hanged and the rebellion subsided, but the legislature had learned its lesson and steps were taken to redress the grievances.

Word of Shays' Rebellion spread through the other states and there was much shaking of heads and muttering of fears for the future.   Also there was growing realization that a central government by a sort of friendly agreement was really not a government at all.

Weak as it was in the places where it should have been strong, principally in the power to control taxation and commerce, the Continental Congress deserves high praise for two pieces of legislation dealing with the so-called Wild Lands between the Appalachian Mountains and the Mississippi River. Here was a vast area practically equal in extent to the thirteen original states. Before the Revolution several of the colonies claimed wide stretches of it on the basis of grants in the original charters.   Virginia far outstripped the others in the size of her demands, amounting to the present total of six states, Kentucky, Ohio, Indiana, Illinois, Michigan, and Wisconsin.

There is a paragraph in the second charter of Virginia granted by James I of England in 1609 that is worth reading for all its quaint, old fashioned language:

> And we do also . . . give, grant, and confirm, unto the said Treasurer and Company, and their Successors, under the Reservations, Limitations, and Declarations, hereafter expressed, all those Lands, Countries, and Territories, situate, lying, and being, in that part of America called Virginia, from the Point of Land, called Cape or Point Comfort, all along the Sea Coast, to the Northward two hundred Miles, and from the said Point of Cape Comfort, all along the Sea Coast to the Southward two hundred Miles, and all that Space and Circuit of Land, lying from the Sea Coast of the Precinct aforesaid, up into the Land, throughout from Sea to Sea, West and Northwest.*

The important statement in this pretentious declaration was the last, particularly the phrase "up into the Land, throughout from Sea to Sea, West and Northwest." What seas were those that King James dealt with so generously and vaguely? The first of course was the Atlantic, but what was the other, that sea which was now to be the western boundary of Virginia? Strange as it seems to us today the early guesses as to the breadth of this new land were absurdly small. It was taken for granted that something called the Western Ocean was only a few miles away, up this river, over that hill or mountain. Captains of ships bringing settlers and supplies to Virginia in those first hard years after 1607, in the "starving time," were expressly directed to bring back gold, precious stones, and the way to the Western Ocean. They cruised as far as they could or dared up the rivers of Virginia, the Potomac, the James, the Rappahannock, in the hope that somewhere near would be found the route that would lead them into that elusive sea that must lie beyond the narrow strip of land that was America to them. The stupendous fact that more than three thousand miles of forest, mountains,

*See *Documents of American History,* Edited by Henry Steele Commager, Document No. 7.

plains, and desert must be crossed before the Pacific would be sighted would have been incredible to the royal mind. In the course of time and by common consent and usage the Mississippi River had been accepted as a substitute for that "other sea." The vagueness of the terms "west and northwest" was characteristic of royal generosity. This land was the property of the King; why not give as much as he chose to his loyal subjects in Virginia, although no one knew the immensity of this domain?

Although the charters of other colonies gave less reason for dreams of a western empire than in the case of Virginia, several of them were not slow to follow the example of the older colony and Georgia, the two Carolinas, Connecticut, and Massachusetts laid claim to western lands. The result was a confused overlapping, particularly in what are now Michigan and Wisconsin. Massachusetts did little to back her imperial pretensions except to argue briefly with New York over the title to lands occupied before the Revolution by the Seneca Indians bordering on Lakes Erie and Ontario. Connecticut made more warlike gestures seeking to hold northeastern Pennsylvania round the headwaters of the Susquehanna. She submitted somewhat sullenly when the courts properly named Pennsylvania as the rightful owner and sought recompense in a narrow belt along the southern shore of Lake Erie, establishing a feeble outpost under the leadership of Moses Cleaveland where the flourishing city of Cleveland now stands. Western Reserve was the name given to this westward reaching antenna and Western Reserve University is a thriving contemporary monument to early Yankee hopes.

The states without such extravagant pretensions observed the contest with growing disquiet, especially little Maryland and Rhode Island. Maryland felt herself penned in between Pennsylvania and mighty Virginia and in danger of being ground between these millstones of empire. Her chance to make her opposition felt came when the Articles of Confederation came up for ratification by the Congress. By refusing to vote and thus preventing the unanimous action that was required she was able to postpone a vote for four years, until the year of the capture of Cornwallis.

The solution of the tangle was surprisingly simple. Maryland suggested that the competing claimants should cede their western lands to the Congress "as a common fund for the use and benefit of such of the United States as have become, or shall become members of the confederation or federal alliance of the said states."* New York and Connecticut had acted a year earlier than did Virginia, but it was the action of the latter state that broke the jam. Georgia alone held back and it was not until 1802 that she grudgingly yielded her offhand claim to all the land to the west of her as far as the Mississippi.

So matters stood to the west when the negotiators in Paris finally agreed on the terms of peace with England. The war officially ended and the new government, such as it was, confronted the problem of governing. Bringing the thirteen states together in united action was difficult enough at the best, and with the thorny question of administering an inland empire added there seemed no clear road ahead for the Congress to follow. British troops still held the frontier posts around the Lakes and gave no sign of early evacuation. To the planners in London the future seemed certain. The American colonies had broken away from the sheltering arms of the mother country. So what? There was no longer need to protect colonial trade. England ruled the waves and could easily edge the new nation out of the profitable trade with

*Quoted from the Virginia Act of Session. See Commager, *Documents of American History*. Document No. 76.

the West Indies, which she proceeded to try to do. Meanwhile she had only to sit tight in her guard posts in the West and the fur trade in the Ohio country would be hers. Soon the wayward children would see the error of their ways and humbly petition for readmission into the Empire. The Loyalists who had managed to stay on through the war took heart. Later the English were to learn that American ships and merchants were not to be so easily beaten out of their share of world trade.

Thomas Jefferson was one man who did not share the general confusion and bewilderment. He almost alone, except for a few perennially hopeful land speculators, had the imagination to see a United States that was to be. In 1784, not long after Virginia's surrender of her western claims, Jefferson presented to Congress a plan for the government of the western territory, particularly the area north of the Ohio River. As soon as possible this was to be divided into ten states and he even had names for them, including such classical aberrations as Cherronesus, Assenisippia, Metropotamia, Polypotamia, and Felisippia. These were merely superficial eccentricities of a great mind. The body of the report was sound and to the point.

Congress might hesitate and postpone and doubt the necessity of action in behalf of the West, but settlers and Indian traders did not. By the standards of today the seaboard states were anything but crowded, population was about three million strong along the narrow fringe from Maine to Savannah, fifteen hundred miles, but good land was already hard to find in the older communities. In the first hundred years of our history the movement of people to the westward had been at the pace of a snail, perhaps a mile a year, but it was beginning to speed up. Even during the active fighting, when Washington and his ragged heroes were battling for their lives in New Jersey and around Philadelphia, men singly and in small groups were slipping through the passes in the Alleghenies and the Blue Ridge to see what they could find beyond. These forelopers found danger in plenty, but they also found great forests, fertile valleys, and land to be had for the taking.

Daniel Boone in the Shenandoah listened to the tales of William Finley, woods wanderer, trader and itinerant peddler and preacher, and followed him through the Cumberland Gap into Kentucky, the "dark and bloody ground." In his first lonely year he dodged Indians, lived on the food the wilderness offered in abundance, and looked. The next year he led a small group out of Virginia over the Wilderness Trail that he had blazed on his first trip and built a stockade at a place he called Boonesborough. Here was an earthly paradise, forests, pure cool water, and room for all comers. In the Blue Grass farther west were great herds of deer, elk, and buffalo. The forests held bear. For many years, westward movers could read on a large tree beside the trail a record carved by Boone in the bark attesting that here "D. Boone kiled a bar," one of the very early historical tablets of the American roadside. It was a fair land and one in which only a coward or a shirker need go hungry.

Farther south migrants from southern Virginia and North Carolina, men with such Scotch and Huguenot names as Sevier, Robertson, and Henderson, found what they sought. As early as 1769, while England was trying to convince the colonists that the West was temporarily closed until the people in London could get around to organizing it, a cluster of log cabins calling itself Watauga had appeared in what is now northeastern Tennessee not far from Knoxville. Soon after the Revolution a young man from North Carolina named Andrew Jackson joined them. By 1784 when Thomas Jefferson was working on his plan for the organization of the western

lands a new commonwealth called the Republic of Franklin
was functioning spasmodically in the valley of the Tennessee. About the same time Richard Henderson, speculator
in land and politics, was proclaiming an organization in Kentucky that he hoped would be the free state of Transylvania. In
the city of Lexington, Kentucky, today there is a monument to
Henderson's vague dream in the shape of Transylvania University, the first college to appear west of the Alleghenies. The
year that this daring institution made its appearance was 1780,
Cornwallis was still at large in Virginia and the outcome of
the war was still in doubt. Whatever was in men's minds in
London, Paris, and Madrid, and even in Philadelphia, the
American people were on the move westward.

These new Americans faced a common danger — Indians.
This trans-Allegheny country was the home and the hunting
ground of able, large, and warlike tribes, Creeks and Cherokees
in the south, Shawnees in Ohio and Kentucky, and Iroquois in
the north. The last named, probably the ablest and certainly
the most feared of them all, had guessed wrong on the Revolution when they cast their lot with the British and when the
war ended all but a scattered fragment were moved by the
British authorities into upper Canada. There the town of
Brantford in the province of Ontario perpetuates the name
of their famous leader Joseph Brant, once the protégé of Sir
William Johnson, onetime Indian Commissioner for the British and holder of a princely domain in the Mohawk Valley of
New York. After the war ended the Johnson estate was
taken over by the State of New York and sold in small parcels
to settlers, the fate of other lordly holdings in the New World.
Shawnees, Creeks, and Cherokees distrusted all white men,
whether American or British, and stood guard over their cher-
ished ground. It was not until after the War of 1812 that
their strength was finally broken.

It was in 1785 that the Congress finally deciphered the writing that was appearing on the map of the West and passed an "Ordinance for ascertaining the mode of disposing of Lands in the Western Territory." This law, one of the most important in our entire list of laws, provided a system of surveying land to permit easy location and sale. The area north of the Ohio was to be divided into townships six miles square, each township to be given a number, from south to north beginning at the point on the Ohio River where the western boundary of Pennsylvania terminated. Range lines were to be run from east to west. They were also numbered progressively with Range One starting at the point indicated on the Ohio and extending to Lake Erie. This process was to be repeated as the surveyors worked westward until the whole region had been cut into neat numbered squares. The basic unit for purposes of sale was to be six hundred and forty acres known as a *section,* so that each township contained thirty-six sections. Provision was made for reserving Section Sixteen in each township for the support of public schools. Provision was also made for the sale by townships and sections to individuals or groups of settlers at a uniform price of a dollar an acre.*

This old land ordinance laid the groundwork of government land policy for the next eighty years and fixed a system of survey that was to march with us to the Pacific Ocean. It had the beauty of definiteness and made the overlapping of claims practically impossible. Now the public land was being measured and described ready for the buyers. There the framers of the Land Ordinance had guessed badly. They knew what had happened in the early days of Massachusetts when groups

*By way of illustrating this method of survey, the author was born on a small farm in western Illinois described as "the East half of the Northeast quarter of Section 29 in Township Twelve north, Range one, West of the Fourth Principal Meridian, in the Tract appropriated for Military Bounties in the Territory of Illinois."

of people, often the members of a particular church, had petitioned for a grant of land somewhere near Boston where they might settle and build a church and a school as the nucleus of a township. It was thus that Watertown, Belmont, Concord, Sudbury, and many others had begun, guardposts against the threat of Indian attack. The price the settlers had paid was the labor of clearing the land and building their houses. But that had been a hundred and sixty years ago and there was no Boston in Ohio to serve as the center of a ring of frontier settlements. But the price named in the ordinance was a dollar an acre and the Congress was hoping to sell whole townships, thirty-six sections, or at the least a section of six hundred and forty acres.

Most of the westward movers were young and a Conestoga wagon would easily contain all their worldly goods and gear and they had no money. To ask such people to put down $640.00 in any kind of cash was to ask the impossible; besides a section of land, most of it covered with trees that must be cleared away, was far more than they wanted or could use. They had an answer to the terms set by the government for the purchase of public land. They would take it without deed or payment. This was public land and they were the public. The Penns had had large experience with "squatters," as they were called. Nearly a hundred years earlier James Logan, the Penn agent in Pennsylvania, had complained bitterly that there were almost as many of these free riders on Penn land as there were paying tenants. The squatter was to be a continuing problem to the government land office until the passage of the Homestead Act in the midst of the Civil War eighty years later. Speculative companies appeared to bargain with Congress for large tracts for which they proposed to pay in depreciated Continental currency sometimes as low as nine cents an acre. The Ohio Associates was one of the most prominent among these optimistic gamblers. They asked for five million acres and finally settled for less than a fifth of that quantity. Individual offers were few and the land offices did little business.

With the ending of the war and the increase of interest in western land it became evident to the Congress that people on the land called for some sort of government. The result was another important piece of legislation by the otherwise feeble and dying Congress. This was the famous Northwest Ordinance, officially called "An Ordinance for the government of the Territory of the United States northwest of the River Ohio." The date of the passage of this act was July 13, 1787. This was the swan song of the Continental Congress. If it had done nothing else in the fourteen years of its existence the Congress would still deserve our grateful remembrance for this Act. Briefly it laid down the foundations of our system of territorial government as an apprenticeship for statehood. Provision was made for the appointment by Congress of a governor and secretary of the district and also of the necessary number of judges. When a district could show a population of five thousand a territorial legislature was to be chosen by the people to enact laws dealing with purely territorial matters. Each territory was entitled to send a delegate to Congress who could debate laws affecting the territories, but without the right to vote. This was to be a temporary probational status aimed at statehood when a territory had reached a population of sixty thousand. The total number of states northwest of the Ohio was fixed at not less than three nor more than five. In his "Report of Government for the Western Territory" three years earlier Jefferson had suggested ten. The Northwest Ordinance determined the manner in which new states were to be added to the Union and only Texas and California were exceptions.

This device of a territorial interlude was a neat means of avoiding the humiliation of a colonial relationship under which the original Thirteen had suffered so long.   Here were no royal governors or governors' councils ruling by royal favor or with the permission of a distant Parliament, but a free people learning by experience to govern themselves.   Its long success has amply demonstrated the wisdom of the act.

CHAPTER XIV

We "Revise" the Articles of Confederation

Before the ink was dry on the Treaty of Paris it had become increasingly evident to thoughtful Americans that winning the war had not been enough. The first paragraph of the treaty signed in Paris, September 3, 1783, declared:

> His Britannic Majesty acknowledges the said United States [Here the names of the thirteen states are given] to be free, independent, and sovereign states; that he treats with them as such, and for himself, his heirs, and successors, relinquishes all claims to the Government, proprietary, and territorial rights of the same, and every part thereof.

These were cheering words to the men who had followed Washington through the hard years, but they offered no guide to the future. Much as they had resented the colonial status, it had at least provided a form and method of united government. If they were ruled unjustly, it was a uniform injustice. British laws of trade had seemed oppressive, but colonial merchants had been skillful in evasion and colonial trade had offered large profits, especially in the West Indies. Now they were thirteen independent sovereignties, each with his own rights and sense of destiny.

During the war there had been one main problem for the colonists, winning their freedom from British rule. Now there were as many problems as there were states; there were even more than that — the new lands to the west with their growing population. In January of 1787 Dr. Benjamin Rush, able physician and devoted patriot, spoke with a prophet's tongue in his "Address to the People of the United States," when he said: "The American war is over; but this is far from being the case with the American Revolution. On the contrary, nothing but the first act of the great drama is closed. It remains yet to establish and perfect our new forms of government; and to prepare the principles, morals, and manners of our citizens, for those forms of government, after they are established and brought to perfection."

Few local leaders were as gifted with foresight as was Dr. Rush. For too many of them this was an opportunity for the individual state favorably situated as a trading center to feather its own nest. Consider the case of New York. The thrifty burghers there had done fairly well for themselves during the Revolution and now they had a free hand. Their harbor was the best along the entire coast, well sheltered from storms with deep water up to the wharves and plenty of anchorage room. The near neighbors, Connecticut and New Jersey, found there the natural market for their products, chiefly foodstuffs. Their necessity was New York's opportunity and the good burghers pushed through legislation establishing customhouses with all the machinery of inspection, taxation, and control. Other ports strove to imitate New York, but none could equal her.

Mention has been made of boundary disputes in which most of the colonies were involved. The Continental Congress was authorized to settle these; the Articles of Confederation said so, but the Congress was on its last legs and knew it. Many delegates had abandoned even the pretense of regular attendance and the respect in which the body was held had practically disappeared. The debts were growing steadily as unpaid interest was added to principal and the Congress was powerless to do anything about it. It was a government without legislative, executive, or judicial authority except as these were provided by the separate states. Each seaport town set up its own rules of trade, naturally giving itself all the breaks possible. The "firm league of friendship" declared by the Articles of Confederation was rapidly becoming a discordant chorus of bitter rivalry and ill will. In his *Observations on the Commerce of the United States* Lord Sheffield in Parliament envisioned the monopolization of American overseas trade by English ships with none of the costs and hazards of colonial government. "America can not retaliate. It will not be an easy matter to bring the American States to act as a nation. They are not to be feared as such by us." There was every reason for such gloomy prophecy, but there was little prospect for an effective revision of the Articles of Confederation. Out of the Revolutionary fighting had come not one nation but thirteen, apparently ready to fly at each other's throats.

In this dark time a long-standing quarrel between Virginia and Maryland over the exact location of the line between the two came to a head in a meeting of representatives of the contending parties as guests of George Washington at Mount Vernon. The point at issue had to do with the drawing of a line on water. In the earlier negotiations little Maryland had put a fast one over on big Virginia and the bargainers had fixed the line well over toward the Virginia side, thus leaving the navigable channel mostly in Maryland territory. Now that state was threatening to close the river to Virginia ships, thus proving that a river is not a "natural" boundary but a highway, a lesson that the world has been slow to learn, especially along the Rhine and the Danube.

Virginia knew the answer to that and called attention to the fact that she held the two capes, Charles and Henry, on opposite sides of the mouth of Chesapeake Bay. Incidentally she still does. If Maryland closed the river to Virginia traffic she would do likewise to Maryland at the mouth of the Chesapeake, shutting Maryland off from free access to the Atlantic Ocean. Clearly this was a game in which neither side could win and the conferees at Mount Vernon, being sensible men, took the sensible course of fixing the boundary where it belonged, in the middle of the navigable channel of the river.

This happened in 1785 and the incident set a few men, notably Alexander Hamilton in New York, to thinking. Why not a general meeting of representatives of all the states to thresh out their respective differences in friendly fashion, instead of shouting loudly at each other in legislative assemblies and in the newspapers? The next year such a general meeting was attempted at Annapolis, but to no apparent purpose. The states were slow to learn and only five sent delegates to the Annapolis meeting. Among them were James Madison of Virginia and Alexander Hamilton of New York, two men who were both wise and persistent. One of them, it is not known which, seized the opportunity to propose a meeting in the spring of 1787 of delegates of all the states "to take into consideration the situation of the United States, to devise such further provisions as shall appear to them necessary to render the constitution of the federal government adequate to the exigencies of the Union, and to report such an act . . . . . . as will effectually provide for the same." It was voted to send this communication to the legislatures of the respective states and also to the Continental Congress.

A congress is by nature prone to debate and delay and correspondingly slow to act so it was not until February 21, 1787, that the dilatory Congress got around to the request; by that time seven of the states, led by Virginia, had appointed delegates to a meeting, if and when such a meeting of all of them should be held. The resolution finally passed was characteristically vague and cautious. The meeting was to be held in Philadelphia:

> on the second Monday in May next, [May 14] for the sole and express purpose of revising the Articles of Confederation, and reporting to Congress and the several Legislatures such alterations and provisions therein, as shall when agreed in Congress, and confirmed by the States, render the Federal Constitution adequate to the exingencies of Government, and the preservation of the Union.

By such slow and guarded steps did our forefathers move toward the setting up of a government that might really govern. The meeting that was thus called for May 14, 1787, is of course known to us now as the Constitutional Convention.

On the date set for this meeting for the "sole and express purpose of revising the Articles of Confederation" not enough states were represented by delegates to form the quorum necessary for action and it was not until May 25 that the convention opened with nine states reporting as present. Only one delegate from New England had appeared even then, Rufus King of Massachusetts who was to be one of the useful men among the delegates; the absentees were New Hampshire, Rhode Island, Connecticut, and Maryland. New Hampshire sent no delegates until late in July. Rhode Island was suspicious of the whole idea and sent no delegates at all. That New Hampshire finally turned up is to be set down to the credit of John Langdon, the richest man in the state, who paid the expenses of the other delegate, Nicholas Gilman, who came with him. During the Revolution Langdon had paid the expenses of a brigade of militia at the battle of Bennington, raising the funds in part at least by mortgaging his silver plate and a large cask of port.

The delay of eleven days was not entirely wasted time. Systematic, punctual James Madison of Virginia was among the early comers and looked over the room chosen in the Pennsylvania State House, now known as Independence Hall, and selected a chair for himself. He tells the story in his famous Journal, our only reliable and complete account of the proceedings, all of which were secret with guards at the doors to turn away curious visitors. Madison records: "I chose a seat in front of the presiding member with the other members on my right hand and left hand. In this favorable position for hearing all that passed I noted in terms legible and abbreviations and marks intelligible to myself what was read from the Chair or spoken by the members; and losing not a moment unnecessarily between the adjournment and reassembling of the Convention I was enabled to write out my daily notes during the session or within a few finishing days after its close." Then he adds with a delightful air of casual afterthought, "It happened also that I was not absent a single day, nor more than a casual fraction of an hour in any day."

The convention had an official secretary, William Jackson of South Carolina. Mr. Jackson had served usefully during the Revolution, a lieutenant in the Continental Army before he was eighteen and a major at the end, but as a secretary he was near to being a total loss as his notes were confused and almost undecipherable. Nothing of the sort could be said of the Journal kept by Madison. Here was one of the most, if not the most, useful men in the room. A graduate of Princeton and a sedulous student all his life, no one in the country had a better understanding of political history and theory than he. His Journal was no accident; it was typical of the man.

When the Convention was finally opened the list of delegates present held twenty-eight names representing nine states, enough for a quorum competent to begin the work. Prominent among them of course was George Washington of Virginia.

He had hesitated to serve because of the pressure of work on his plantations, neglected through the years of war. When he bade farewell to his officers in New York and turned homeward he had hoped that his public service was at an end. It had been a long time since he had led the Virginia militia with Braddock in the tragic march on Fort Duquesne, more than thirty years punctuated with frequent calls that could not be denied, Virginia House of Burgesses, Continental Congress, Commander in Chief of the Continental Army which he was expected to raise, equip, and lead. Surely he had served out his time and might be permitted to retire into the life he loved the most on his Virginia farms. Now in Philadelphia in this year 1787 he was the most marked man in the group and it was inevitable that he should be elected as president of the Convention. He was in his fifty-sixth year.

Next to him in world-wide fame was Benjamin Franklin, best known American in London and Paris, chief figure in the negotiations in Paris that had led to the Treaty of Alliance, wise, tolerant, and patriotic. Without his patient, persistent urging French aid might not have come at all, or come too late. He was the conciliator of the Convention whose wise counsel held the discordant elements together more than once when failure seemed certain. There is a legend that on one such occasion when tempers were strained to the breaking point Franklin proposed that a clergyman be called in to seek divine aid. The legend goes that this was done, angry feelings became tranquil, and the proceedings more orderly. Something of the sort happened, according to Madison's Journal, but not quite as the legend has it. Franklin did offer a resolution to that effect, but non-religious Hamilton, after asserting his profound respect for his venerable friend and for his great services to his country, expressed his fear that if it became known that the delegates were in such despair that

they were reduced to asking divine aid the result would be a
general weakening of public confidence.   Another delegate
called attention to the fact that there were no funds for the
payment of the clergyman.   There was no second to Franklin's proposal and the matter was dropped.

Franklin spoke seldom and then briefly and usually with
humor.   One useful contribution came near the end of the
long sessions when the discussions were being prolonged and
confused by the unwillingness of some of the delegates to yield
on minor points of opinion or prejudice.   Then he told of the
remark of a crochety old French woman to her sister: "I
don't know how it is, Sister, but I meet with nobody but myself that's always in the right."   His listeners laughed and the
tension eased.   He was the oldest man in the Convention,
eighty-one.

Next to him in age was Roger Sherman of Connecticut
who was sixty-six. Sherman in his youth had been apprenticed
to a shoemaker, but he had educated himself and at this time
was a judge in New Haven and had been elected mayor of
his adopted city for life.   Shrewd and prudent, he was plain
in speech as in dress; his most useful contribution was in the
discussion of the method of electing the members of the two
houses of Congress, the Great Compromise.   It was Sherman
who hit upon the plan of choosing members of the lower house
by popular vote and of the upper by the state legislatures. He
was one of the useful men at Philadelphia.

With the exception of Franklin and Sherman, it was a
gathering of young men.   Madison was thirty-seven, Hamilton thirty, King of Massachusetts thirty-two, Gouverneur
Morris of Pennsylvania, aristocrat, wit, social favorite, thirty-
five; the youngest delegate was Jonathan Dayton of New
Jersey, twenty-seven.   Of him contemporary opinion sug-
gests that youth was his only contribution to the meetings.

The average age of all the delegates was forty-two. Our Founding Fathers were wise, but certainly not venerable.

Not all the delegates were prominent men, in fact many of them were unknown outside their own communities, but not all the prominent Americans were there. Thomas Jefferson was in France as Minister, John Adams was in London trying to wind up the tangled skeins of the Treaty of Paris. The first volume of his *Defense of the Constitutions of the United States* was published that year. His cousin Samuel, the firebrand of the Revolution, failed of election as a delegate and was not too ardent in his support of final ratification. John Hancock was another Massachusetts name that was not on the roll. Christopher Gadsden of South Carolina, an aging radical who "feared leaders more than he feared Tories," was not chosen but later he turned conservative and supported ratification. Patrick Henry, orator and spokesman for the frontier counties of Virginia, unfriendly to the ideas of the tidewater planters, declined to consider election, probably from a desire to be in a position to oppose the decisions of the Convention; at least he later opposed ratification. He would have been a colorful figure in the long sessions but of doubtful value otherwise. In fact in the state convention to consider ratification later he was once on the edge of a duel with Governor Randolph whom he charged with betrayal of his own principles.

The delegates as a whole represented the educated, property-owning elements in the seaboard cities. Of the total of fifty-five who finally appeared, however briefly, in the sessions, thirty-one had been students in college, here or overseas. Much has been made of the hard lot of the debtor in dealing with the creditor and it must be said that in general it was the creditors who were represented in the convention.

Luther Martin of Maryland was the chief, if not the only, spokesman of the "under dog" in many of the discussions.

There were frequent references to the opinions, hopes, and fears of something called "The People," but it may be doubted that many of the disputants had more than a sketchy understanding of the masses of the population. Democracy as we understand it today found little favor in 1787. All thirteen states had property qualifications for voting, the most common being land or its equivalent of the value of a hundred dollars. Since most of the adult men except laborers in the larger cities owned land this was not so burdensome as it appears at first glance. A few of the states, notably South Carolina, had a much higher requirement for holding office. In that state senators must have land to the value of two thousand pounds sterling.

Professed atheists and members of non-Christian bodies were barred. In Connecticut only members of the "state church," the Congregational, could vote or hold office. Other states were content to require belief in a "doctrine of rewards and punishments," in a future life of course. Illiteracy varied, low in New England, high in the South and on the frontier where there were few schools, even poor ones. Several of the delegates favored wealth as the measure of representation in the central government, wealth to be determined by the contribution of the state to the common cause. These men remembered only too well the laggard performance by some during the Revolution. This suggestion lost popularity after a powerful speech by James Wilson of Pennsylvania attacking the doctrine that property was the prime purpose of organized society. Not wealth, said Wilson, but the "cultivation and improvement of the human mind," adding that a majority of the people must always control the minority, or government will become impossible. After this little was heard of property as the basis of society or the measure of representation.

The total population at this time was around three million as was shown by the census of 1790. The largest state was Virginia with nearly seven hundred and fifty thousand, almost three hundred thousand of them slaves. Delaware was the smallest with 59,094 and 887 slaves. That tiny state had had a variable history having been by turns a Dutch, then a Swedish, and finally an English colony claimed by Pennsylvania and known as the "Three Lower Counties on the Delaware." Generations later this circumstance would move Senator Ingalls, witty, cynical senator from Kansas, to refer to Senator Bayard of Delaware as "my distinguished friend from that state which has three counties at low tide and only two at high." It had appeared first as one of the thirteen as late as 1776 when it claimed and secured the right to separate representation in the Continental Congress.

Of the cities Philadelphia was admittedly the largest with 42,000 as against New York's 33,000 and Boston's 18,000. Charleston with its 16,000 population, was the only metropolis south of Baltimore. Philadelphia was not only the leader in numbers and probably in wealth, but it was also a cultural center, a condition to which Benjamin Franklin had made notable contributions. The Library Company was his work as was the Academy that was the germ of the present University of Pennsylvania. Printing and publishing flourished with a changing procession of newspapers and magazines. The year of the Convention a company of players came over from New York and gave a series of performances known as "concerts" to avoid censure from those who regarded the "strolling player" as merely a polite term for vagabond. The hall in which these "concerts" were given was called the Opera House, also to allay prejudice. Shakespeare may have been mistaken when he declared that a rose by any other name would smell as sweet.

Philadelphia also had some good taverns and one, the "Indian Queen" near the State House, became the favorite lodging place and rendezvous of delegates. The landlord reserved a common room for the exclusive use of the delegates where they spent many evenings in talk and conviviality. Here too the rule of secrecy applied and no word of the many spoken there in these out of hours sessions leaked through to the outside world. Probably James Madison wasted little time in these "bull sessions."

The opening meeting of the Convention began in a pouring rain. Little more was done than to elect a President, Washington, and choose a secretary. Neither of these matters produced discussion nor did the decision to held the meetings in secret. The sensible men, and there were several of them, knew that they were facing a long and complicated task, and not holding a series of debates for the edification of the public. At one point in a long wrangle over ways of compelling the states to obey the laws passed by the national legislature, Gerry of Massachusetts proposed that the provision should be written in language that the people would not understand, "to save them from alarm."

It should be noted that Mr. Gerry's name has passed into our political vocabulary. When the time came to divide his state into Congressional districts he took an active part in drawing the district boundaries, having a wide knowledge of local political views and habits. An observer viewing the map that resulted commented on the strange shapes there exhibited: "That looks like a salamander," he said putting a finger on one part of the map. Another, knowing Gerry's part in the making of the weird pattern, remarked: "Say rather 'Gerrymander!'" To this day to "gerrymander" is to redraw the district boundaries in such devious ways for party advantage.

Reporters might be barred from the Convention meetings, but there was no law against guessing. On July 19, when the delegates were beginning to doubt the possibility of an outcome of any kind except an admission of failure, the *Pennsylvania Packet,* published in Philadelphia, blandly announced: "So great is the unanimity, we hear, that prevails in the Convention upon all great Federal subjects, that it has been proposed to call the room in which they assemble Unanimity Hall!"*

Early in the sessions Washington warned his colleagues of the difficulties they faced. "It is too probable that no plan we propose will be adopted. Perhaps another dreadful conflict is to be sustained. If to please the people, we offer what we ourselves disapprove, how can we afterwards defend our work. Let us raise a standard to which the wise and good can repair. The event is in the hand of God." At least that was as Gouverneur Morris remembered it twelves years later in his memorial oration after the death of Washington. It might well be true.

The Virginia delegation held several of the men most prominent in the discussions, especially James Madison, George Mason, Edmund Randolph, the Governor of the state, and for a short time George Wythe, perhaps the ablest lawyer in the new nation. It was Mason's hard lot to refuse to sign the finished document in September because of its lack of a Bill of Rights, later corrected by the first ten amendments. He was of unquestioned aristocratic origin as was Randolph. Mason's great-grandfather had fought for the King in the long struggle with Parliament in England and had commanded the King's

*Cf. *The Great Rehearsal.* Carl van Doren. Viking Press.

cavalry in the battle of Worcester. Wythe was the teacher of both Thomas Jefferson and Henry Clay in their study of law.

It was typical that this group should bring with them to Philadelphia a plan for a constitution ready to present. Such subjects as the form and attributes of government were meat and drink to Madison, Mason, Wythe, and their acquaintances, and their opinions and proposals were definite and challenging. Randolph presented the plan on May 29 and the first fortnight of the meeting was largely devoted to its discussion. This Virginia Plan has been described as a series of proposals intended to alter, or "revise," the Articles of Confederation as much as possible, contrasting with the "New Jersey Plan" offered by Paterson of that state on June 15, which was an attempt to change the Articles as little as possible. This is an oversimplification, but it contains considerable truth. At least the Virginia Plan contained many of the basic elements which were to reappear in the Constitution as finally adopted. Here they are:

1. The national government should consist of a legislature, an executive, and a judiciary. This was in line with the practice of most of the states.

2. The legislature should consist of two houses. This too was standard practice in the states, although Pennsylvania was then experimenting with a legislature of only one house.

3. Election of the members of the "First Branch," now the House of Representatives or the lower house, by popular vote. It was proposed, however, that the members of the "Second Branch," now the Senate, be elected by the members of the First Branch.

4. A National Executive to be created, to be chosen, however, by the National Legislature.

5. A National Judiciary to be established consisting of supreme and inferior tribunals.

6. Provision to be made for the admission of new states.

7. A Republican form of government to be guaranteed to each state.

The Virginia Plan was read to the convention in formal session and then referred to the "Committee of the Whole" for detailed consideration and later reported back to the convention as revised. The term "Committee of the Whole" refers to a device often used to permit the fullest freedom of discussion and also test votes, which are not binding on the convention in formal session. The membership of this committee is identical with that of the convention as a whole, but a special chairman is chosen, doubtless a welcome relief to Washington who was thus permitted to be merely among the delegates present. It is interesting to note that Madison records only one speech by the dignified and silent president in the course of the entire convention. Gouverneur Morris of Pennsylvania made 173, Wilson, also of Pennsylvania 168, Madison 161, Sherman 138, Mason 136, Gerry 119.

Morris, the man of many speeches, was a bizarre figure in that serious gathering, more of an eighteenth century English aristocrat in dress, manners, and morals than a colonial American. His mother had remained openly loyal to the motherland and his brother held a commission in the British Army and was married to the Duchess of Gordon. The Morrisses had large estates and big houses, but there was never any doubt of the patriotism of this one. There were scandalous tales whispered about his wooden leg with hints of an outraged husband and a hasty leap from a high balcony, but the reality was less romantic, only a prosaic runaway of his carriage horses and a clumsy surgeon who chose amputation in preference to setting a compound fracture. His portraits reveal him as a full-bodied gentleman with a wide sensuous mouth, full lips, and drooping eyes. He was thirty-five years old in the year of the Convention.

The fear of the smaller states lest they be overwhelmed by the larger was a marked feature of most of the earlier deliberations. In the Continental Congress the rule was voting by states, one state one vote, whatever the number of delegates. The ratification of the Articles of Confederation had been delayed for three years by the refusal of Maryland to vote either way until the disposition of the western lands had been determined. Now little Delaware, a newcomer in this turbulent family, felt herself in a peculiarly dangerous position, a feeling shared by New Jersey and Maryland to a considerable degree. The fear was so marked in Delaware that the legislature in choosing delegates had imposed upon them a binding condition to withdraw from the convention if any change in the Confederacy rule of equality in voting was even considered.

The division between large and small states was not always obvious or logical; usually, however, the list of the large began with Virginia and included Pennsylvania, Massachusetts, the two Carolinas, and Georgia, although the last could hardly be regarded as even settled. Georgia was still hoping that she would be permitted to hold all the land west of her as far as the Mississippi and felt herself at least potentially large. In New York most of the territory in the Mohawk Valley west of Albany had only recently been wrested from the Iroquois, late allies of the British. Massachusetts held the Province of Maine and was sparring with New York for a share in the area bordering on Ontario and Erie.

New Jersey felt herself to be in an uncomfortable position. During the war she had been a battleground hemmed in between Philadelphia and New York and ravaged by both sides. Now she sought to find a way of escape from her commercial dependence on those two cities. New York was the natural market for the agricultural products of her northern counties and New York had imposed a tax on imports, especially those from the other states, and New Jersey was the victim nearest at hand. For all the bombast in the certificate of one of the state's delegates, "William Livingston Esquire, Governor, Captain General, and Commander in Chief in and over the State of New Jersey and Territories thereunto belonging," she was weak and small and naturally became the chief spokesman for her small neighbors. Incidentally Georgia was not exactly modest in her designation of herself in the certificates of her delegates in Philadelphia, "The State of Georgia, by the grace of God, free, sovereign and Independent." One of her delegates bore the title of President of the University of Georgia, an institution not yet in existence.

Much of the discussion in the early sessions revolved around this watchful jealousy among the states. The truth was that many of them were strangers to each other and to the other states. Madison frankly admitted that he knew no more of the affairs of Georgia than of those of Kamchatka. On coming into Philadelphia many of the southerners thought of themselves as adventurers in a foreign and perhaps unfriendly country. One of the Pinckneys from South Carolina made public admission of his surprise and pleasure in finding the people of the North as friendly and hospitable as those of his own land.

At long last, on July 17, the men from the large states, fearful of adjournment as a confession of failure, agreed to drop their demand for a proportionate representation in the Senate, as in the House, and settled for equality of voting power among the states in the upper chamber. So it was agreed: the Senate represented states, the House people. Election of senators by the state legislatures remained the rule until

1913 when the amendment providing for the election of senators by popular vote was adopted.

This was the crucial point in the long and sometimes vehement sessions. It was a hot summer and the convention sat for five to seven hours a day six days in the week. It was little wonder that patience and tempers wore thin. At the same time, July 17, final agreement was reached on the length of term in each house, two years in the lower and six in the upper, with one third of the senatorial terms expiring every two years. There is a story that Jefferson breakfasting with Washington once asked him why he supported the longer term in the Senate. In answering Washington asked his guest why he poured his coffee into his saucer. Jefferson, taken by surprise, said, "Why, to cool it of course." "Exactly," said Washington. "The Senate is the legislative saucer in which the hot liquid brewed in the other house is cooled." It probably never happened, but more than once later events have proved the aptness of the characterization.

There were many proposals for the manner of choosing the chief executive, the length of his term, his eligibility for reelection, and the definition of his powers. Most of the delegates had active recollection of life under a king and his royal governors and there was little likelihood of experiment with a limited monarchy, but might not a powerful president become a king? Edmund Randolph of Virginia argued for a dual executive, each watchful of the other. Several spoke for an advisory council, perhaps from the Senate. How long should a president serve? There was strong support for a six year term, without eligibility for reelection. Others suggested service for life, or good behavior. One satirical suggestion was a twenty year term as that seemed the "median life of princes."

Finally, as though wearied by the unending swirl of suggestion, opposition, warning, and exhortation, the Convention decided upon a term of four years with nothing said about further eligibility. The manner of choosing the executive produced much less debate, probably because there was no strong support for a popular election. That was a point on which there seemed little doubt; whatever the manner chosen, the decision should not be in the hands of the democratic mass. As we know, the final decision was for a group of electors nominated by the state legislatures. This can hardly be said to have worked at all, although the form still exists and the voter, hardly aware of it, still votes for electors instead of candidates. The election of Washington was obvious and inevitable. To choose anyone else as the first president would have been ridiculous. When John Adams was in the White House as the first occupant of that structure, congressional and legislative caucuses appeared with their favorite candidates; finally came political parties with conventions, candidates, and platforms. That important development took place in 1832.

The performance of the Convention on the choice and function of the chief executive was somewhat less wise and perceptive than usual. To the delegates democracy was a synonym for licentiousness and parties would be nothing but warring factions. As little power as possible should be left to the people and the government they planned should be in the hands of the good, the wise, and the well to do. They were the proper custodians of security, order, and property. Even Jefferson, who has been described as a Democratic-Aristocrat, believed that political power belonged rightly to those who had a "stake in the community," stake meaning landed property.

It was the coming in of new states that troubled the placid waters of their dream of harmony and progress. There was little discussion of such a possibility although there were faint proposals that new states should not be permitted to outvote the original thirteen. The final clause admitting new states contains only eleven important words, "New States may be admitted by the Congress into this Union. . . . ." The phrasing was the work of Gouverneur Morris, who was charged with the responsibility of putting the document into finished literary form for signing. Later in a letter to a friend he admitted that he purposely left the provision for new states vague in order to permit later action to define and limit. New states came too fast for further editing. Vermont, Kentucky, and Tennessee, before the century was out, and each of these came in with full manhood suffrage, except for slaves. Here was a force that not even the Founding Fathers could foresee or prevent.

The Judiciary brought out little controversy or bitterness. The need for a Supreme Court was clear to most of the delegates, although there was a widespread feeling that its duties would be light; but should there be inferior courts? Many of the delegates thought that the existing state courts would take care of all the cases that were likely to arise, with occasional appeals to the higher tribunal. How should Supreme Court justices be chosen? There were arguments for appointment by the Senate or by the President, but none for popular election, although that was the method followed by some of the states. The irrepressible Franklin cited a practice that he said had once prevailed in Scotland where judges were chosen by members of the bar who generally selected the best lawyer and put him on the bench in order that the other lawyers might divide his practice among themselves.

So the discussions dragged on through the hot summer with a recess of ten days early in August to permit a Committee of Detail to prepare a report on actions to that date. Washington drove with Gouverneur Morris in the latter's phaeton, "drawn by Washington's horses," to Valley Forge where the Virginian wandered over the site of his old winter quarters of ten years before while Morris, who had no memories of that starvation place, amused himself fishing for trout. Neither one left any observations or conclusions to posterity on that brief holiday, not even the luck of the fisherman.

After reconvening on August 6 the delegates gave their attention to the report of the Committee of Detail which placed before them a substantial framework of government. Paragraph by paragraph they studied the text, on the whole amicably, although there were still a few controversial points capable of producing fireworks. One of these was the proposal to prohibit export taxes by Congress. Madison opposed this as an arbitrary and improper limitation of the power to control commerce. In general the disputants assumed that the states would still possess the right to impose such a tax. In the end it was agreed that states should be denied the right to levy taxes on either imports or exports without the consent of Congress.

Slavery and the slave trade held problems that haunted the minds of several of the delegates throughout the meetings and in the end demanded some kind of recognition. The final action was negative in form, but it stilled the debate for the time being:

> The Migration or Importation of such Persons as any of the States now existing shall think proper to admit, shall not be prohibited by the Congress prior to the year one thousand eight hundred and eight. . . .

That was the late summer of 1787; six years later Eli

Whitney, Connecticut Yankee, built the first cotton gin and the demand for field hands in the fields of the Deep South began to rise. If the time had been six years after the Whitney invention, instead of six before, would the Convention have acted differently?

The Committee had recommended that the right to pass bills appropriating money should be exclusive to the lower house; in the upshot the Senate was given the right to "propose or concur with Amendments."

The final stage was reached on Wednesday, September 12, when the Committee of Style presented an engrossed copy of the completed document. Credit for its "style" was later claimed for Gouverneur Morris, probably with justice. At least few delegates could match him in literary skill. Was Morris also responsible for the changed wording of the Preamble? On this point the records give no answer. The report of the Committee of Detail had read: "We the people of the States of (names of the thirteen in order from north to south, beginning with New Hampshire and ending with Georgia) do ordain and establish. . . ." Now at this last moment of Sept. 12 the delegates saw at the top of the copy before them: "We, the People of the United States, in order to form a more perfect union, to establish justice, insure domestic tranquillity, provide for the common defence, promote the general welfare, and secure the blessings of liberty to ourselves and our posterity, do ordain and establish this Constitution for ourselves and our posterity."

Why the change? Was this a subtle thrust aimed at the sovereignty of the states? In view of the curious controversy over the hidden meaning of this change it is worth while to explain that by this time, September 12, the convention had agreed that ratification of the new constitution by nine states, two-thirds of the total, was sufficient for the moment. The old rule of a unanimous vote as necessary for the amendment of the Articles of Confederation no longer applied. They were bypassing the Continental Congress. Here was no plot, only an acceptance of the realities of the final revolution. There was no dissent or discussion.

The last day of this momentous meeting was a long one, seven hours, from eleven o'clock to six, without recess for food or drink. Delegates were weary and the matters of home called to them peremptorily. It was Saturday, but there was no weekend holiday for these workers. The final vote was twelve "ayes," none opposed. Thirty-nine of them signed; Washington as president of the convention made the total forty. The task was done. Now the people of the states acting through delegates in separate conventions must decide.

While the signing was going forward Franklin made the last speech of the session, as usual mildly humorous, conciliatory, and to the point. On the back of the president's chair was a conventional drawing of a sun. Pointing to this design, he spoke of the difficulty of determining whether the sun there shown was rising or setting. Madison recorded the old man's conclusion: "Now at length I have the happiness to know that it is a rising and not a setting sun." Then the delegates marched in a body to the City Tavern where an elaborate and "elegant repast" was served. From beginning to end they had sat for seventy-nine days, but few of them were faithful in their attendance. Madison missed no meetings and the same thing was true of the silent Washington. The major part of the work had been done by a few men, probably less than twenty.

Here are the names of the men whose part in the discussions can scarcely be ignored: Madison, Washington, Sherman,

King, Hamilton, in spite of long absences, Franklin, Mason, Paterson, Charles C. Pinckney, Rutledge, Randolph, Wilson, Martin. The case for others is at least more difficult to prove. Mason of Virginia refused to sign because of the lack of a Bill of Rights for the protection of the individual. Hamilton was the only signer for New York, one of the critical states. John Lansing, a follower of Governor Clinton of New York, dropped out after six weeks and later opposed ratification. Richard Yates, the third New Yorker, took little part and dropped out July 10. He also opposed ratification. Gerry of Massachuetts explained his failure to sign as due to his fear of civil war in Massachusetts, a fear that few of the other delegates shared.

With the Constitution adopted by the convention, what should they do with it? The meeting had been called together by the Continental Congress for the purpose of revising the Articles of Confederation. To call this sweeping result a revision was a misuse of words too absurd to be seriously considered. It was equally absurd to submit the new Constitution to the Continental Congress for adoption with or without alteration, or for rejection if they chose. To expect the Congress to approve was to expect that body to commit *hara-kiri*.

The Convention voted to submit their handiwork to special conventions in the various states called by the state legislatures for that sole purpose. Of this decision Carl van Doren in *The Great Rehearsal* says: "Here was one of the most revolutionary decisions in the whole convention, and in the long run one of the most practical." At the same time the convention voted that ratification by nine states was enough for adoption. That would make the new government at least a going concern which other states might join later as they chose. No longer would it be possible for one or two stubborn sisters to delay action indefinitely.

The business of ratification proceeded at varying pace in the different states. Little Delaware was the first to act, voting to ratify on December 7; Pennsylvania followed five days later, and New Jersey fell in line on December 18. Before the end of June, 1788, nine states had ratified and the new Constitution became the supreme law of the land, at least for the daring nine. New Hampshire by hard pushing was the ninth, but Virginia, North Carolina, and New York were still holding back. Rhode Island, which had not bothered to send even a token delegate to the convention, indicated her intention of continuing to take no part in this dangerous innovation. In Virginia the influence of George Mason was strong and Patrick Henry attacked the document in fiery words as the death blow to our liberties. Madison fought persistently for ratification and his state came in on June 25, close on the heels of New Hampshire. It was in New York that the most bitter fight was waged both for and against. Governor George Clinton at Albany had under his control a close-knit machine in the Hudson River counties above New York and he came close to threatening secession if the city of New York persisted in its demand for approval.

It was the tactics of the New York convention that brought about the publication of the famous *Federalist Papers*, chiefly written by Hamilton for New York newspapers while the battle on the floor of the convention proceeded. The papers have been highly praised for their wealth of learning, the cogency of their arguments, and their calm, passionless tone, but it is to be doubted if they were as immediately effective as the crushing answers given by Hamilton in the give and take of debate. Much of the argument in the Papers was over the heads of many of the delegates, but for later generations they have become the classic record of the best political thought of the time. When it was finally seen that the

Empire State was in danger of finding herself isolated by her neighbors enough votes shifted to permit ratification on July 26, but by the narrow margin of thirty to twenty-seven.

In North Carolina a strong "back country" opposition to any kind of general government prevented action and a second convention was necessary. The step was finally taken on November 19, 1789. Now only little but important Rhode Island was on the outside, and stayed there until the new Senate of the United States adopted a resolution ending commercial relations between the United States and Rhode Island. On May 29, 1790, Little Rhody grudgingly capitulated but by the hairline margin of thirty-four to thirty-two.

In spite of all that was written or spoken in the state conventions and afterwards on the proceedings of the ratifying conventions and the terms of the final action there still persist vague statements that in this case or that ratification was conditional, permitting later withdrawal if the union proved unsatisfactory. The condition most often mentioned in several conventions was the addition of a Bill of Rights, following the lead of George Mason. This proposal was dealt with in the first ten amendments adopted by the First Congress and ratified without opposition by the states. South Carolina is sometimes mentioned as reserving the right to secede if in her judgment such action was in the best interests of the state. The fact of record is that in the state convention in Charleston the opposition was a one-man affair in the person of Rawlins Lowndes who claimed to speak for the back-country settlers and confined himself largely to praise of the old Confederacy, an argument that found few supporters. Similar statements have been made about reluctant Rhode Island. In the brief and inglorious life of the Eighteenth Amendment it was said that the final surrender of that state was brought about by the promise of the right to withdraw peaceably whenever the state chose.

The stubborn fact is that while many delegates urged many conditions as necessary none of the ratifications was handicapped by special terms. In each case the responsibility was of the "take it or leave it" order, for the simple reason that there was no official body in existence competent to promise or deny. If there was to be change except as provided by constitutional amendment it could only be by insisting on another national convention, and no delegate appeared anywhere with the hardihood to advocate such a course.

The Constitution was the work of wise, devoted men through nearly three months of unremitting labor. They were men, not demigods or angels. What they had sought to do was to establish a government with the power to govern but not to oppress. George Washington had seen the ending of the war that was to be called the Revolution and he had presided over the body that was to bring a new government into being. The War had been won and now the Revolution had been accomplished. The United States of America was a reality.

※※

CHAPTER XV

What Kind of Government Is It?

For all the proposals, objections, and resolutions through that long, hot summer from May 25 to September 15, the final document contained less than five thousand words, not counting the amendments to be added later. A fast reader can go through it in an hour, but to read it with understanding takes a little longer, a lifetime perhaps. It has been in active service for a hundred and seventy years and is still going strong. But what kind of government is it that has lasted through depressions, domestic discord and tumult, great wars and small with less real change than any other government in the world?

To begin with it is a government of United States, not a "firm league of friendship." That is important, as the powerlessness of the loose-jointed Confederacy had amply demonstrated. It was not as powerful as Hamilton had wished, but had the ability to tax and collect. That fact alone operated mightily to establish credit at home and abroad. In the long debates such terms as "national," "central," and "federal" had been used rather indiscriminately. This was not really a federated government since the sovereignty of the separate states had been considerably abridged. The Confederacy had been a federation and there were few to praise it or to mourn its passing.

210

Whatever term one might employ to characterize this new structure, it was also a government of limited powers, with, as far as possible, specific duties and functions. Read the Tenth Amendment:

> The powers not delegated to the United States by the Constitution, nor prohibited by it to the States, are reserved to the States respectively, or to the people.

While this clear statement was not in the body of the instrument as ratified by the state conventions, Madison's notes on the discussions during the summer indicate that it was implicit in the minds of the framers in their consideration of the relations of state and nation. Delegates had an acute awareness of their responsibility to their home states and only Hamilton openly favored the reduction of the erstwhile sovereign states to the status of convenient administrative agencies. It was around this thorny problem of state versus nation that much heated debate revolved, both in the Convention and elsewhere.

Madison, who should have known what he was doing if anyone did, left this as his considered opinion: "The proposed Constitution . . . . . . is, in strictness, neither a national nor a federal Constitution, but a composition of both. In its foundation it is federal, not national; in the sources from which the ordinary powers of the government are drawn, it is partly federal and partly national; in the operation of these powers, it is national, not federal; in the extent of them, again, it is federal, not national; and finally, in the authoritative mode of introducing amendments, it is neither wholly federal nor wholly national."

It was inevitable that out of the background of individual colonial experience in both peace and war should emerge something difficult to classify, at least in European eyes. It was more than a federation and certainly less than a unitary

state. How much more or less time would tell. The dim
specter of States Rights as a fundamental principle of government still walks among us, chiefly in party conventions,
but the flame that John C. Calhoun once lighted around it was
burned out in the hotter fires of Civil War aimed at secession.
Now it is little more than a convenient recourse of politicians
hard pressed for more convincing arguments. The great fact of
1787 was that out of their hard necessities the framers
had evolved a federal government of a kind not known before.
In similar manner in our own time the British Empire became
the Imperial Commonwealth of Dominions, something new
and seeming strange, also the result of stark necessity.

It is sometimes asserted that delegates toyed with the idea
of an American monarchy. Hamilton is charged with a plan
to set a crown on the weary head of Washington, George I of
America perhaps. If such a plan existed Madison made no
record of it. There is a rumor that the president of the mori-
bund Continental Congress, otherwise a figure of no political
importance, wrote a letter to Prince Henry of Prussia asking
him to consider applying for such a post. Another name
that has been mentioned was that of the Secular Bishop of Os-
naburg, in civil life Prince Frederick Augustus, Duke of York,
second son of George III. These were empty rumors. Madison's notes gives no hint of time wasted by such impossible ex-
pedients.

It was early decided that this was to be a three-headed
government, Legislative, Executive, Judicial, with clear division of function and power. It is often called a government of
checks and balances, but this is hardly the case. It can more
truthfully be styled a government of complementary and
limited powers in which Legislators legislate, Executives ad-
minister, and Judges sit in judgment. All three branches have

limitations set to their powers and there is a large area in which the individual is greater than any government, federal, state, or local. These men had had enough of absolutism in their colonial days.

That the new government should be one of limited powers was obvious to the members of the Convention, but definition of the limits was not so obvious. Clearly the government should be adequate to provide for those matters that were purely national; at the other extreme the states should have exclusive control over those matters which were undeniably of state concern. This was so obvious that to say it was to say nothing. Where was the line between the extremes to be fixed and by whom? Here the framers sought to draw up a list of items that were to be within the competence of the Congress, including some of the things the national legislators might not do. Out of this came the Tenth Amendment which has been quoted above. Out of this came also the conclusion that this was to be a government in which the national powers and functions were delegated and all rights not so stipulated should be reserved to the states or to the people. That sounds simpler than it has proved to be in actuality. There is interstate commerce, for example, over which the Congress was to have jurisdiction. Fair enough, but trade has become more complicated with the appearance of far-reaching corporations of widely distributed ownership and operations, and successive decisions by the courts have broadened the term until, as hostile critics have been prompt to point out, most businesses above the dimensions of a peanut stand are engaged in interstate trade.

The first President who attempted to draw the line sharply between delegated and reserved was Thomas Jefferson and it was his lot to railroad through the purchase of Louisiana,

practically doubling our national domain, without a hint of
constitutional right or authority. But Jefferson was a strict
constructionist seeking to exercise only the powers delegated
to him by the Constitution. Circumstances alter theories as
well as cases.

The Convention had given long consideration to the
manner of electing and the function of the Chief Executive. The colonial experience had given most Americans of
that time a profound distaste for powerful executives. The
constitution of the State of New Hampshire had made no provision for a governor at all, hoping that the president of the
General Assembly would serve their purpose. There was a
general belief that the legislatures, state and national, were the
best guardians of freedom, so they put their trust in Congress. This new government was to be primarily a Congressional government if they could make it so, of course with due
regard for executive and judicial dignities. Actual experience
was to make us aware of the fact that powerful Presidents in
times of great emergency, such as war or depression, tend to
use their powers to the fullest and a little beyond. The sus-
pension of the writ of *habeas corpus* and the stretching of martial law to cover cases not primarily within the jurisdiction of
the military authorities during the Civil War offer cases in
point.

The space devoted to the judiciary in the text of the finished document is less than a page of fine print. Nothing is said
therein about the power of the Supreme Court to declare an
act of Congress, or of the President, unconstitutional, but two
or three references to such action in the convention debates
on the judiciary strongly suggest that possibility. How else
could the Court exercise its function to keep watchful ward

over the foundation stone of the new structure? It was unfortunate that the first decision declaring the right of the Court to pass on the constitutionality of an act of Congress, written by Chief Justice Marshall in *McNary v. Madison,* should have had a rather tawdry setting of political revenge obscuring the real issue of judicial supremacy.

Viewed from the standpoint of a hundred and seventy years of use it is clear that the experiment of a definite written constitution under judicial guardianship is the unique feature of our government, coupled with the combination of federal and state rights. The question is often asked, "Is this then a republic or a democracy?" The answer is that it is both, largely republican in the method of operation through representatives, basically democratic in its choice of such representatives by popular vote. The determination of eligibility to vote, the fundamental expression of democracy, lies with the states. Hence we have had such apparent paradoxes as woman suffrage in one state, Wyoming, and in no others and at the present time men and women voting at eighteen years of age in one state alone, Georgia.

The Declaration of Independence with its proclamation of separation from England and its assertion of the right of the governed to alter or abolish their government when in their judgment it ceased to be conducive to the proper ends of government represented the extreme leftward thought of the time. It was in essence a radical document. The framers of the Constitution, on the other hand, were avowed foes of radicalism. Now the pendulum had swung back to the right and the Constitution is the working demonstration of that swing. Effective frames of government are not to be struck off in a white heat of revolutionary fervor. These were lawyers, business men, property owners, men of substance concerned to set up a machine that would work. They were by nature and interest conservative and the government they created is essentially conservative. That is the basic pattern of our Constitution within the limits of which all changes and reforms must be kept. To ignore this is to ignore the Constitution itself.

What was the political philosophy that was expressed by the Constitution as viewed by its framers in 1787? Probably almost any of the delegates would have called it conservative-republican, a term that may still have some meaning. There were many references in the debates to what the "people" thought or wanted or feared, but there is little to indicate that the speakers knew or cared greatly about what we today call public opinion. To most of them the word "democratic" was a term of reproach. In all of the states there were property, and, in many, religious qualifications for voting or holding office. Jefferson's ideal society might have been described as an agrarian republic with few specific powers.

It was the unexpected increase in the number of new states and the rapid growth of population that soon determined the location of the ultimate political power. The Convention walked gingerly around the question of sovereignty in the discussions, although the Articles of Confederation had clearly placed it in control of the signatory states. Today it is as clearly in the hands of the people. Voting is an act of sovereignty, however microscopic the share held by any individual may be. Any attempt to restrict the suffrage is foredoomed to failure. Conservative we may still be and probably are, but the foundation of our government is democratic.

From Concord to the Constitution was only thirteen years. In that time, short as history goes, independence was asserted, a war won, and a revolution accomplished. In 1775 the population of the new nation was approximately three million and the area only the narrow fringe of thirteen colonies along the Atlantic coast. Now we are crowding a hundred and eighty million and we are scattered through fifty states. In spite of all the amending and interpreting the Constitution is still the Supreme Law of the land. In a chaotic world we have been able to keep house in a stable and enduring environment. We are still doing it!

INDEX